£85

Maris Piper

120

Remove before
cook...

Navel

M 0805 865 S

**Perfectly Ripe
Large Avocado**

M&S
EST. 1884

4509

M 0903 318 S

Peru
1J3105C1

Valencia

M 0805 865 S

**Ripen at home
Avocado**

Allow to ripen out of the fridge
Once ripe store in the fridge

1✗07/2021

M&S
EST. 1884

PERU
4508

M 0356 831 S

**Perfectly Ripe
Large Avocado**

M&S
EST. 1884

PERU
4508 DON

M 0903 318 S

1J02T0C1

FIRST
THROUGH
THE
CLOUDS

FIRST THROUGH THE CLOUDS

THE AUTOBIOGRAPHY OF A BOX-KITE PIONEER

FREDERICK WARREN MERRIAM
FOREWORD BY PHILIP JOUBERT

AIR WORLD

AIR WORLD

FIRST THROUGH THE CLOUDS
The Autobiography of a Box-Kite Pioneer

First published in 1954 by B.T. Batsford Ltd., London.
This edition published in 2018 by Air World Books,
an imprint of Pen & Sword Books Ltd,
47 Church Street, Barnsley, S. Yorkshire, S70 2AS.

ISBN: 978-1-52672-616-2

A CIP catalogue record for this book is available from the British Library.

Printed and bound by TJ International Ltd, Padstow, Cornwall
Typeset in 11/13 Palatino

Pen & Sword Books Limited incorporates the imprints of Atlas, Archaeology,
Aviation, Discovery, Family History, Fiction, History, Maritime, Military, Military
Classics, Politics, Select, Transport, True Crime, Air World, Frontline Publishing,
Leo Cooper, Remember When, Seaforth Publishing, The Praetorian Press,
Wharncliffe Local History, Wharncliffe Transport, Wharncliffe True Crime and
White Owl.

For more information on our books, please email:
enquiries@pen-and-sword.co.uk,
write to us at the above address, or visit:
www.pen-and-sword.co.uk

Contents

Foreword to New Edition by Nick Stroud   vii
Foreword by Air Chief Marshal Sir Philip Joubert KCB, CMG, DSO   ix
Preface   xi

Chapter 1   Wonderland Flight   1
Chapter 2   How It Started   3
Chapter 3   Early Birds   9
Chapter 4   A Shaky Solo   14
Chapter 5   Revolutionary Methods   19
Chapter 6   Some Early Crashes   25
Chapter 7   A Fruitful Year   29
Chapter 8   Never a Dull Moment   33
Chapter 9   The Price of Knowledge   39
Chapter 10   My First Bad Crash   48
Chapter 11   Best in the World   53
Chapter 12   Piling up the Hours   58
Chapter 13   Chingfliers   61
Chapter 14   First Zeppelin Raid   68
Chapter 15   Quality Before Quantity   75
Chapter 16   Airborne Again   82
Chapter 17   Down in the Drink   87
Chapter 18   A Word About Blimps   92
Chapter 19   Sea-Plane Joy Flights   97
Chapter 20   Birth of the Bureau   104
Chapter 21   Back in Navy Blue   111
Chapter 22   Past, Present and Future   116

Index   125

Foreword to the New Edition

By Nick Stroud,
Editor, The Aviation Historian

It is almost impossible now to imagine a world in which the sound of progress was the gentle clip-clopping of hooves rising from loitering country lanes, when the staccato rat-tat-tat of the first primitive aero-engines and the whistling of wires in wings overhead was cause for celebration — or cursing. It is this bucolic idyll that provides the backdrop for Frederick Warren Merriam's lyrical memoir of his early days as a pioneer flying instructor, an occupation which brought unforgettable moments of sheer exhilaration and joy, but which was also stalked by tragedy and grief.

It was reading *First Through The Clouds*, originally published in 1954, and its previously unpublished companion volume, *Echoes from Dawn Skies*, that kindled my admittedly late-blooming interest in early aviation, a subject which, for me, has paid handsome rewards the more I've explored it. If you know little about those pioneering aerial adventurers (like I did — and probably still do), this is a perfect place to start; if you're already familiar with the adventures of Merriam and his band of "maniacs" — his own words — then this will be a welcome reissue of a hitherto hard-to-find British early aviation classic.

We're delighted to be able to assist in the republishing of this wonderfully evocative account of "those magnificent men in their flying machines" (and it's worth noting that much of that enjoyable film was based on the exploits of Merriam and his merry band), thanks to the author's granddaughter Sylvia Macintosh and her family, who have kept the author's journals, manuscripts and invaluable photographs in immaculate order since the pioneer's death in 1956.

Let the adventure begin, with our hero standing beside the hangar at Brooklands in 1912, looking towards the clouds and pondering what lies within …

Nick Stroud,
Editor, The Aviation Historian,
September 2017.
www.theaviationhistorian.com

Foreword

By Air Chief Marshal Sir Philip Joubert
KCB, CMG, DSO

For those who learnt to fly in England before the 1914-18 War, Warren Merriam's book *First Through the Clouds* must awake much interest and evoke a severe attack of nostalgia – the smell of burnt castor oil, polluting the fragrance of a summer dawn as the Gnome engines were starting up; the anxious eyes on the tree-tops watching for the first sign of a breath of wind that would put a stop to instruction until perhaps the evening calm made possible a resumption of activity; the first circuit with the instructor, the cautious landings and the thrill of the first solo. All these are recalled by Merriam's story of his flying experiences. He rightly claims to have taught a large number of officers and civilians and taught them so successfully that the majority have survived to this day or have died in their beds.

He himself had a number of narrow escapes, and once at least he took an involuntary bath in the Brooklands sewage farm. One of my more mirth-provoking recollections is the sight of him emerging – black, dripping and stinking – after a little monoplane that he was flying had crashed into one of the filter beds. Even on this occasion, his usual good humour did not desert him. I think it was probably this side of his character and his infinite patience that made him a good instructor. His determination to go on flying in spite of failing eyesight and official discouragement makes this book good reading for young pilots or for those who intend to take up flying as a career, and who may feel handicapped for one reason or another. It is also a worth-while contribution to the history of flying in Britain.

Autumn, 1953

Preface

In this book I have attempted to give an account of a period in my life which was concerned with some of the most interesting events and personalities in the world of flight from its early infancy to the middle of the last war. My aim in writing it has been to fill some of the gaps in the history of British aviation and to convey to the present generation the joys and thrills as well as the struggles and sorrows of the pioneering days. I have also tried to show how much the progress of flying owes to individual effort in the past and how important it is that individual enterprise should be encouraged today.

Though my memories of this period are still very vivid, I have taken pains to check them and to supplement them where necessary by reference to the detailed records I have kept since 1911. This has been the labour and pleasure of many years, yet I doubt if this book would ever have been completed had it not been for the devoted and untiring help given me by my wife. To my 1912 Brooklands pupil, Brigadier R.M. Rodwell, A.F.C., and to my Publisher I also owe a debt of gratitude for their valuable assistance and guidance. Lastly I would like to thank the many friends whose encouragement has so often inspired me to continue when I was on the point of "stalling".

Pressure of space has reluctantly obliged me to omit any mention of many of my pupils and colleagues, and for this I hope they will forgive me.

Lieutenant Commander Frederick Warren Merriam AFC, FRAeS,
Southampton, Autumn, 1953.

Chapter 1

Wonderland Flight

Early in 1912 I stood outside the hangars and deliberated. It was on one of those mornings when the land is shrouded in the damp cold of a thick canopy of low mist-like clouds that reduce visibility to a few hundred yards and fill the heart of the eager learner with gloom. Up to this time I had never heard of any pilot attempting to fly through the clouds. Bereft of the aid of a single instrument and the most simple meteorological data, we had assumed from the beginning that flying aeroplanes was possible only when in sight of the ground. In the clouds not only would we lose sight of our familiar earth, but in them we might also meet air conditions of a strange and even fatal nature. Yet to some of us the very uncertainty and imagined danger of the clouds was a challenge.

It would be dangerous to try, I thought. No one but a fool would attempt it. And then, after giving myself no chance to retreat, I blurted out my intention to climb above the cloud and clambered into my machine. There was a chorus of "I'm with you Merriam", but on such an adventure I would not take the risk of carrying a passenger. I took off and started to climb. Visibility was even less than I had thought, and almost immediately I became completely enveloped in the clammy vapour. A leather jacket protected my body, but my trousers soon became saturated. Earth and sun were lost to view and, with them, every fixed mark that had guided my waking life since the day I was born.

Before this, even in the darkest night or densest fog, I had felt the solid ground beneath me. Never had I felt more alone. I had to depend solely upon balance and instinct – the two things the modern instructor will never teach you to rely on – yet the curious thing about it all was that I was quite confident of my ability to fly blind. Perhaps, if the clouds had been thicker, my story might have had a different ending; but after 500 feet or so I could see it was getting lighter. Then, with a breath-taking suddenness, I found myself emerging into brilliant sunshine with the infinite blue sky above. I was stunned by the grandeur and beauty of the scene before me as I scudded along the top of the soft, white, feathery plain. The sun was warm and vitalising, and I felt as if I could have flown on and on into eternity.

By confining myself to flying in small circuits I tried to eliminate the danger of getting outside the area of the aerodrome, but after being above the clouds for several minutes, I realized that nevertheless I might miss the aerodrome and that I had been out of sight long enough to cause some anxiety to those below. Very reluctantly, I pushed the nose down and began to descend. Much to my delight and relief on coming out of the clouds, I found myself right over the hangars. When I landed it was difficult to convince those who were waiting in the cold below that a few minutes before I had been revelling in heavenly sunshine, and not until I had taken two pupils up to see for themselves would they believe that such a thing was possible.

More than any other, it was this wonderful experience, I think, that first put into my mind the idea of one day recording my flying life so that thereby I might perhaps convey to a later generation not only the sorrows and struggles, but also the joys and triumphs of the air pioneer.

Chapter 2

How it Started

My first attempt to leave the ground was in 1886 when, at the age of six, I successfully balanced myself on my father's penny-farthing bicycle. Later I built a pair of stilts twelve feet high and staggered about until I had mastered the art of balance. But when I climbed on to the roof of a three-storey house by way of the drain pipes and guttering and had to be rescued by the fire brigade, it was clear that heights were destined to play an important part in my life.

Balancing and heights had always fascinated me, although – strangely enough – my eyesight was so bad that it necessitated operations and endless hospital treatment, with resulting neglect of school work. I filled in much of my spare time practising balancing and juggling feats with such success that I was told by the world famous juggler, Paul Cinquevalli, whom I met in Manchester, to take up stage work. It might then be thought strange that I should have started my career in my father's saddle- and harness-making business. I loathed it. There was not enough "go" about this sort of business to engage my interest for any length of time, though it was ironical, but perhaps consequential, that I should later become acutely interested in the "horseless" carriage.

After a few years in the saddler's trade and other pursuits I became acquainted with an American, Mr. Olin Lane Merriam, who had come to England to study and collect historical literature. Our friendship ripened, and I eventually decided to leave my father's business to join in partnership with Merriam at Falmouth. There we bought a private house from which we carried on business as book and antique dealers. Merriam was many years my senior, but such was the bond of friendship between us that in 1901 I changed my name by deed poll from Frederick George Warren to Frederick Warren Merriam. Had it not been for romance stepping into the picture in 1902 I might have carried on with Merriam in this trade for years, but the girl who was to become my wife claimed sufficient of my attention to cause Olin's displeasure. This eventually resulted in the dissolution of our business partnership but, happily, not our friendship. He returned to America after generously leaving me the means of continuing business on my own.

It was not long before the desire for a more adventuresome kind of life became too strong for me, and I "side-slipped" from book and antique collecting into petrol engineering and motoring, which were then in their infancy. In 1902, after buying one of the first Triumph motor-cycles, I went to London to purchase a 9 h.p. De Dion car from Mr. Gamage, of Holborn. This little car had only a single-cylinder engine, and I was rather dubious about its ability to climb the Cornish hills with a full load. Together with my father, a Mr. Sam Walley and Mr. Gamage's driver, I made a test trip to Hampstead which convinced me that the car could climb steep hills provided one was prepared to approach the worst ones backward – the reverse gear being lower than the forward gear. Later, I found that when the passenger load was unusually heavy or the hill exceptionally steep it was necessary not only to go up the hill backwards but to get out and push the last bit.

The thrill of that first car! It caused a sensation wherever I drove it.

Having built a garage with an inspection pit and other conveniences, I engaged an engineer with a knowledge of nuts and bolts but little of engines, and we proceeded to dismantle the car completely. I wanted to learn all about the works, and I did! We had to reassemble both car and engine several times before we got them to work again. Running costs were high. Though the car licence cost only 15s., a single Michelin outer cover cost £9. That was not long after the days when a man with a red flag had to walk in front of a motor-car as a warning to the public. The condition of the roads was shocking. Dust, grit, and loose sharp flints all took their toll, and a lot of driving time was wasted repairing punctures and tinkering with the engine while passengers just sat and waited. Another great

4

handicap was the many halts caused through shying horses. I had a method to overcome this which worked quite well after a time. I would stop the engine of the car when approaching a horse, get out and walk nonchalantly over to the animal. I would then pat it affectionately and, after murmuring a few "sweet nothings", would lead it to the bonnet of the car. Having satisfied its curiosity after a few sniffs, the horse would usually pass calmly by, but some horses were too nervous to be coaxed in this manner, which meant that either they or I would have to retreat.

I began to drive for hire and was soon touring all over Cornwall with pleasure parties. People were anxious to be in the vogue, and I experienced some amusing incidents with my passengers.

My most nervous passengers were two elderly spinsters who engaged me to take them to the opening of the Marconi Wireless Station at Poldhu, Cornwall, by the Prince and Princess of Wales (later King George V and Queen Mary). Soon after we had started from their house they asked me to stop the car and, although I assured them I had emergency brakes, begged me to let them walk down the hill. I did not tell them that I was far more worried about climbing the hills than going down them. The villages on the way to Poldhu were gaily festooned with flags and streamers. As we approached we were greeted with noisy cheers and excited wavings, and, when I saw the police pressing back the eager crowds, I realized they must be taking us for some of the royal party. My two elderly spinsters were delighted. On the way back we decided to take a quieter route; but unfortunately the hills were steeper, and on one of the worst the old bus refused to climb – either forwards or backwards, and the ladies had to return by train. Very gallantly, they promised they would not breathe a word to anyone about this misfortune in case it should "prejudice my motoring business".

After many exciting experiences in Cornwall I travelled farther afield, advertising in advance the time of my arrival and the fact that I would give pleasure runs. There was always an eager crowd awaiting. Bristol people were exceptionally keen and kept me there for some time. One name in Bristol stands out very clearly in my memory: that of Mr. G.J. Biggs. He lived at Cotham and came very near to adopting me at one time.

Together we had many drives and quite a number of close shaves. Once we skidded on the tramlines after rain, mounting the pavement and actually running for some way on two wheels. The passengers, seeing me hanging over the side in an effort to stop the car from overturning, luckily followed suit and so got us back safely on all fours again. Amusing incidents, too, were not lacking. One day while I was stranded with engine trouble in Buckingham Palace Road near the Palace, I found it impossible to continue working on the engine because of the many curious onlookers who had collected and were crowding round the car. By managing to get the engine running sufficiently well for my immediate purpose and by the simple expedient of shorting the ignition on to the chassis I gave the hangers-on such an electric shock that they hastily cleared away and left me to complete my adjustments in peace.

By 1904 – the year of my marriage – I was becoming well known in the motoring world, and in the following year was acknowledged by the De Dion manufacturers as a specialist on their cars. They recommended me to Sir Reginald H. Cox, then of Cox's Army Agents, who had just purchased a new car from them. I was engaged to teach Sir Reginald to drive and to tour abroad with him for his health. I then sold my own De Dion to Gould Bros, of Exeter for £140 – £40 less than I gave for it – which was not a bad deal considering the experience and fun I had enjoyed. We took the new 15-20 h.p. De Dion over to France from Southampton, landing at Le Havre, and then motored to Rheims. After this followed a grand month's tour through the lovely French countryside as far as the German frontier. Motoring was much farther advanced in France than in England, and motorists were submitted to a very severe road test. Even foreign visitors had to pass it. But there were advantages. There was nearly always a motor mechanic available in towns and most hotels catered for motorists.

They were wonderful days, and when I look back I sometimes think what a grand career I might have made out of motoring. However, my life was to change completely when that young cycle repair expert, Orville Wright of Dayton, Ohio, one day took a deep breath, pulled back the joystick of his home-made contraption and hopped a few feet into the air. In a moment the motorcar had become ordinary, and I was filled with the urge to fly. I felt that the curtain was up on the first act of a new age – the air age.

Until Orville Wright made his epic flight I had not given much attention to the early efforts of the pioneers. I had heard accounts of the Henson aeroplane and John Stringfellow's experiments five years later, but the thought of actually flying myself was then beyond my wildest dreams. My first desire was to go to America, as Griffith Brewer and Ogilvie had already done, but, my marriage making that impossible, I had to confine my activities to a close study of aeronautics. Experiments with gliding models and observations of bird flights soon taught me quite a lot about air currents and landings. It was knowledge which was later to come in very useful.

Owing to my wife's delicate health I did not disclose my desire to see the flying demonstrations which the Wright Brothers had started to give in France; neither did I let her know that, I, too, was anxious to take up flying. Her death in 1909 at the age of twenty-six was a tremendous shock, and I was left with three children all under five.

The preparation of plans for my children's future occupied me for some months. While this was going on I heard about A.V. Roe's and Moore-Brabazon's successful flights, and, as my plans were completed, there came the sensational announcement that Louis Blériot had won the *Daily Mail* £1,000 prize with his flight across the Channel from Calais to Dover. Knowing that my children's future was now assured I decided to make the plunge. In a few weeks I had come to terms with the British and Colonial Aeroplane Company – now the famous Bristol Aeroplane Company – and had contracted to give my engineering experience to the Company and to pay them £50. In return for this they were to teach me to fly.

To obtain the Royal Aero Club's aviator's certificate at the Brooklands School of the Company (Figure 4) then cost over £100, irrespective of living expenses during training. Army and naval officers paid £75, which was refunded by the State if they were afterwards accepted by the Royal Flying Corps or Royal Naval Air Service. I was well pleased with the terms, but Mr. H. Delacombe, the aeronautical advisor to the Company, eyed me dubiously though not unsympathetically when I proffered my money. He was reluctant to take it and reminded me of the risk I was running both with my money and my neck! It was kindly advice, and I was grateful to him for his sincerity; but I was so keen to fly that nothing could possibly have altered my mind. I might mention at this stage that such was the attitude of some families towards those of their kin who thought of taking up flying that I was compelled to live under an assumed name and to keep my movements secret. For this reason I re-adopted the name of Warren, thinking that my family would never now look for me under their name.

All day, and on many occasions, late into the night I worked hard in the sheds with the mechanics, learning everything I could about the Gnome and Anzani engines and helping with repairs. Then at last came that eventful day which, to this very moment, stands out so vividly in my memory, when the chief instructor took me for my first flight. At long last I was airborne.

Chapter 3

Early Birds

Before I describe my own further adventures in the air I would like to pay tribute to the happy band of men with whom I became associated and whose example sustained my determination to forsake everything for flying. I came to know many of them intimately, and I followed their subsequent careers with as much avidity as the modern youngster pursues those of his film or sporting idols.

Although A.V. Roe was not officially credited with having flown until after Moore-Brabazon, he had in fact been making hops successfully a number of months earlier. On June 8th 1908 – according to eyewitnesses – his machine was airborne several times for a distance of about 75 and 150 feet. [Evidence now points to all these hops not having taken place.]

Previous books on flying during this period have seldom paid sufficient tribute to the early flights of Piffard, Barnes, Howard T. Wright, J.W. Dunne and Rolls. Dunne was the first man to design and fly a V-shaped aeroplane with fully swept-back wings. He is perhaps better known to a growing number of the more intellectual members of the present generation as the author of several highly interesting works on the subject of Time. When the first official flight was made all these men were "hopping" about in homemade contraptions and taking incredible personal risks.

In 1909 the Short Brothers, Horace, Eustace and Oswald (Figure 5), had begun building aircraft. Oswald's interest in flight went back to 1898, when he made his first balloon ascent. In 1900 he designed his first balloon envelope and by 1910 had produced the design for the first rigid airship – "Mayfly". As early as 1904 Horace and Eustace

9

Short had given a joint lecture to members of the Royal Aeronautical Society on the possibilities of ascents by balloon to hitherto undreamed-of heights. They spoke in terms of a spherical metal globe for the passengers equipped with a hand-operated pump for maintaining the air supply and pressure inside. They were thus already anticipating the use of pressurized cabins for the stratosphere flights of the future. Oswald Short also designed, built and exhibited at Olympia his "Silver Streak", a forerunner of the stressed-skin construction which was later to revolutionize aviation. In 1921 his design for a fighter sea-plane to follow the "Silver Streak" was described as impossible to build, but subsequent years were to show that Oswald Short's only fault was that of being yet another inventor before his time. I cannot emphasize too greatly the Short Brothers' contribution to aviation.

England owes much to the genius of Henry Farman, the builder of the Farman box-kite which proved such a worthy instrument for instructional work. Most of our pilots in the years before the First World War obtained their aviators' certificates on Farman box-kites. Indeed box-kites held their place for this purpose until they were superseded by the Avro 504, eventually built in larger numbers than any other plane of that period. It was on a box-kite – a Voisin Short biplane pusher called "Bird of Passage" – that Moore-Brabazon learned to fly (Figure 7). His example inspired several of our own pioneers to go to France to learn as he had done. "Bird of Passage" certainly earned her name, for she passed from one owner to another very many times before her end. Moore-Brabazon's claim to be the first Englishman to make an actual flight was officially recognized by a committee of investigation set up by the Royal Aero Club, with Lord Gorell as Chairman and Messrs. H.E. Perrin, G. de Havilland (Figure 6) and Lockwood Marsh as members.

It was a near thing between Moore-Brabazon and A.V. Roe. A.V. was one of the earliest to start flying at Brooklands; he was also one of the first to sample the joys of landing in the sewage farm alongside the aerodrome. But many more were to follow him there. At that time progress was measured by the length of a hop rather than a flight, and A.V. was often referred to as "Roe – the hopper". He was one of the first to realize that, when taking off, the tail should be raised as speed was gained. Most pilots "stalled" their machines on taking off by having their tails on or near the ground and the nose of the machine in the air. Until they learned better, there were many take-off crashes.

In 1912 A.V. built the first cabin machine. In 1913 he produced the famous Avro (504) which became the standard training aeroplane for the Royal Flying Corps and, later, the Royal Air Force. The 504s were very easy machines to fly, but were sufficiently sensitive on the controls to teach care; they thus became known as the "airman's ideal". In Figure, 8 A.V. is seen flying his triplane at Lea Marshes, Essex. The machine was called the "Yellow peril" because of the colour of the wings, and his workshop was under a railway arch.

The first Blackburn is shown in Figure 10. As were most of our successful pioneers, Blackburn was an engineer. In 1908 he designed, built and flew this monoplane, which was powered by a 35 h.p. Green engine with a chain-driven propeller. This machine was not altogether successful. It left the ground on the first attempt but side-slipped on the turn, crashed on to the ground and was wrecked. Blackburn, fortunately, was not injured, and the mishap spurred him on to further efforts. He later built and flew the all-metal military biplane – the first of its kind – which was to lead to the initial success of the aircraft firm bearing his name.

I am reminded here of one of Blackburn's pupils – Mr. B.C. Hucks – the brilliant stunt pilot who, on a Blackburn monoplane made the first British crossing of the English Channel and was the first Englishman to loop the loop. During this flight Hucks received a wireless message. It was the first to my knowledge to be received by an airman while flying.

Figure 11 shows Colonel S. Franklin Cody, an Anglo-American who became a British subject and who was given an honorary rank by King George V. Clever and daring, Cody had a charming personality. In his early years he was attached to a "wild west" cowboy troupe and then for a time turned his attention to melo-drama. Later he gave up the "Boards" for kite flying and worked on his idea for man-lifting kites, following the same line of thought as that of Dr. Benjamin Franklin, American scientist and statesman of the eighteenth century, who, while flying a kite one day, decided to have a swim in a nearby pond. So, he tethered the kite to the ground and allowed it to remain flying in a powerful wind.

Whilst swimming, however, it occurred to him to see if the kite would draw him along in the water if he held the cable. He found

11

that it would. Cody attempted to tow boats across the Channel with monster kites. The army authorities were so convinced of the utility of his man-lifting kites that they awarded him £500. They also awarded him their £1,000 prize for the best British military aeroplane. Partly because of its size and partly because of its Gothic "architecture", it was affectionately known as the "Cathedral". Cody knew very little about the theory of his work, but that never seemed to worry him. One day, wanting to test the strength of his latest product, he asked three or four of us to go up with him. Three did go, but, not wishing to offend Cody by a direct refusal, I made myself scarce at the time of take-off. This kindly and remarkable man was planning to build an even larger "Cathedral" when he met his death. His plane broke up in mid-air, and his passenger was killed with him.

Sir T.O.M. Sopwith is seen in Figure 12 in his Howard-Wright box-kite, powered by a 50 h.p. E.N.V. engine. It was the type of aeroplane on which most of us learned to fly at that time. Among his pupils then were Major Hugh Trenchard, Capt. E.L. Ellington and Mr. Harry Hawker. Sopwith never mixed with us other aviators. We used to put it down to his shyness; but, whatever the reason, he was a fine pilot, steady and reliable. Outside the Brooklands School of Flying he was really the only pilot of that time with whom I cared to entrust myself. When he took me up I felt quite at ease.

Undoubtedly the most conspicuous flying personality in those days was Mr. Claude Grahame-White (Figures 14 and 15). Inspired by Blériot's epic flight across the Channel, he bought a Blériot monoplane and assisted in erecting it at Blériot's factory in France. With the valuable knowledge this gave him, he began trials at Issy-les-Moulineaux and was soon in full flight. Before he acquired Hendon aerodrome, where he opened his famous flying school, Grahame-White had won many prizes and gold medals in this country and America, but not without involving himself in a number of crashes.

At Eastchurch, Mr. Francis McClean was deeply interested in flying. Early in 1910 he made a patriotic offer to lend two of his Short machines to the Admiralty for training naval officers, and to the acceptance of this offer the Royal Naval Air Service owes its foundation. The first four officers to learn to fly on these machines were Lieuts. R. Gregory, C.R. Sampson and A.M. Longmore, of the

Royal Navy, and Capt. E.L. Gerrard, R.M.L.I. They were instructed, free of charge by Mr. G.B. Cockburn. In 1912 McClean was the first to alight on the Thames – near the House of Commons. His machine was a Short pusher equipped with floats.

This then was the setting of the stage when eventually in 1911 I decided to join the Bristol Flying School of the British and Colonial Aeroplane Company in preference to joining Robert Blackburn, whom I had previously contacted in 1910. The pioneer "chicks" had just begun to topple out of their nests, and the more daring were making their first uncertain flights into the unknown.

Chapter 4

A Shaky Solo

My first taste of the air with the chief instructor, Mr. Collyns Pizey (Figures 16 and 31), more than fulfilled my expectations. Flying was like being transferred from a badly sprung car to a motor-boat. There was such buoyancy in the air that I immediately lost that sense of nothingness or giddiness which I had always felt previously when looking down from a great height. My tuition started right away under conditions which today would be considered appalling.

There were no safety-straps, covering or other protections to offer any security or comfort to the pilot or passengers. All we could do was to hold on to the upright struts with one hand, grasp the joy-stick with the other and trust to providence that we were not thrown out by a violent motion of the machine. The school machines were Bristol pusher biplanes (box-kites) fitted with a 50 h.p. Gnome rotary engine between the main-planes and the tail (Figure 2). They flew at an air speed of about 36-40 m.p.h. and carried 19 gallons of petrol and 9 gallons of oil, sufficient for about three hours' flight. We used to boil sago as dope for the wings, and this made the fabric as tight as a drum.

To learn to fly, a pupil had to have a quick brain, for at that time his only instruction was from his close observation of the pilot's actions and his own common sense. When the weather was calm – "not enough wind to stir a feather" – a pupil would be allowed to hold the joystick over the instructor's shoulder. If he happened to be short in arm or leg, this was a very awkward procedure. Much of the instruction would actually be given on the ground after landing, when the pilot would explain to the pupil what he had been doing in the air. An early stage of our practical training was learning to "taxi", "taxi-ing" being the name we gave to the process of moving an aeroplane about on the ground under its own power. The pupil would then sit in the pilot's seat, and, with the instructor sitting behind him, would learn to control the machine by the rudder bar and by "blipping" the engine on and off with the switch on the control column.

When all was said and done, it was mostly a case of the blind leading the blind. The qualified aviator of those days could only just wallow about in the air himself and had little real knowledge of what he was doing. Flying was a dangerous business then. Aeroplanes were constantly breaking up in the air – let alone on take-off and landing; there were no parachutes and the pilots were ever expectant of mishaps. But the spirit of comradeship engendered among us was ample reward for the dangers faced. When there was a bad crash, and often when there was a minor one, everyone rallied to the rescue, including those in the rival sheds. Then, too, conferences were often held between rival factions on the aerodrome to discuss ideas and to exchange opinions. Tools were loaned and borrowed, and there was none of the jealous rivalry which was to mark later years of commercial competition.

Soon the proud day came when Pizey told me it was time for me to make my first straight flight (Figure 17). The news travelled quickly around the aerodrome, tools were downed and everyone turned out to watch the fun or to assist, if necessary, with the wreckage, and it was the usual thing for observers at these flights to lie on their backs on the ground to see to what height the machine rose. Pressmen were always on the spot, for we usually made good copy.

I took off in great style, but the habit of switching off and on while taxi-ing, which had so thoroughly been instilled into me, returned at the wrong moment when I was landing. I switched off thirty feet up, and only in the nick of time did I switch on again.

The Aeroplane of that time records the event with the words: "Warren (Merriam) also entered solo flying stage. At first attempt at landing switched off too soon, machine began to pancake, so with great presence of mind switched on again and made an excellent landing."

After considerable practice on "straights" I was detailed to make my first circuit at a height of 200-300 feet. I had the "wind up" properly. I was fearful also that if the machine was damaged I might spoil my prospects of becoming an instructor with the firm. I took off safely, making sure not to switch off my engine this time, and proceeded to carry out my circuit; but in my excitement I overlooked the instructions to reach a height of 200 feet before turning and kept throughout the flight perilously near the ground. Having hit one or two air bumps which banked the machine to a steep angle, I was anything but happy when I turned in, narrowly missing the Blue Bird chimney-pots, to float halfway across the aerodrome and finish up within inches of the railings. It was the custom of dear old Pizey to hide in the Blue Bird Restaurant near the starting-point while a pupil carried out his first circuit. There he would stay until someone came in to tell him it was all over. He could not bear to witness these ordeals, and, when I look back, I can realize just how nerve-racking they must have been for instructors. What a sigh of relief I heaved as I sat in the machine and saw Pizey come running out! He was deathly pale, for it gave him a nasty turn when he heard the noise of the engine as I skimmed the roof.

He sent me off again to make a better show, but once more I was drawn towards the Blue Bird. How I missed it the second time I don't know, and it was only by luck that I stopped again before hitting the railings. This time I felt too ashamed even to face Pizey. I knew what he must be thinking of my two rotten attempts. But, to my surprise, he was only mildly angry. I think his anger was overcome by relief at finding that the machine and I were safe and sound.

After my first feeble efforts I am sure everyone expected me to finish off the Blue Bird at my next attempt; but, after a trip as passenger with Fleming, I put up quite a good show. Fleming briefed me carefully where to land, and the circuit went off without incident. It was a wonderful feeling to have flown a circuit alone and landed safely, particularly when there were so very few other pupils able to do the same. How Mrs. Billing, the proprietress of the Blue Bird managed to survive the strain of these solo flights is a mystery. She was a marvellous woman, attending to all our minor injuries, darning our socks, and even cheerful when faced with the latest ravages of the sewage farm.

After this I was fully occupied with left- and right-hand turns, figures of eight and landings at a given spot. This was the final stage in the process of qualifying for the Royal Aero Club aviator's certificate. The actual test involved two distance flights of at least 3 miles 185 yards each in a closed circuit and an altitude flight, minimum 164 feet, which had to be a separate flight from the previous two. The method of "alighting" prescribed for each flight was that the motor should be stopped at or before the moment of touching ground and that the aeroplane should come to rest within a distance of 164 feet from a point previously indicated by the Royal Aero Club Observer.

I eventually passed my test on February 6th 1912 in a Bristol biplane, with the envied record of having completed my training without damaging a machine. The Royal Aero Club observer was R.L. Charteris, and my certificate was No. 179. I could have taken my test earlier, but my agreement with the firm meant that I – unlike the other pupils – could take my time, and I preferred to wait. It is interesting to note here that Certificates 1, 2, 3 and 4 granted before the official test was brought in – went to Mr. J.T.C. Moore-Brabazon, the Hon. C.S. Rolls, Mr. A. Rawlinson and Mr. C.S. Grace.

The school at Brooklands opened in 1910, and in that year four pupils were granted certificates under the instruction of the French pilot M. Edmond; they were L.F. Macdonald, S.E. Smith, A.R. Lowe and Capt. T.H.F. Wood. About the middle of 1911 Mr. Howard Pixton, who had qualified for certificate No. 50 on a Roe triplane, joined the Company and took charge of the school until Pizey and Fleming came on the scene at the end of the same year.

Just before I arrived at the school Pixton had trained Major R. Brooke-Popham and General David Henderson. During 1911 a total of sixteen pupils obtained their brevets at the school, among them being Harold Blackburn and Lieut.-Col. Frederick Sykes. Roughly half of them dropped out of flying before the war broke out in 1914, and four, at least, were killed. At the end of 1911 there remained a number undergoing tuition, including myself, who all eventually secured their certificates early in 1912. Among these successful pupils were Capt. C.A.H. Longcroft, Major G.H. Raleigh and Major Sir A. Bannerman, Bart. Most of these early 1912 pupils received instruction from me before and after I gained my "ticket". With the exception of three or four, they afterwards disappeared from aviation.

Before I close this chapter I should like to mention just a few of the early Brooklands' civil pilots, some survivors of whom are still engaged in aviation – in the air or on the ground. They remain a fadeless picture in my mind: A.V. Roe, T.O.M. Sopwith, Gordon England, F.P. Raynham, R. Kemp, N.S. Percival, H.A. Petre, W.O. Manning, and F.E.T. Hewlett. The last man was partly taught to fly by his mother, Mrs. Maurice Hewlett, the first woman in this country to become a qualified aviator.

Chapter 5

Revolutionary Methods

In 1912 I disclosed the secret of my role as aviator to my parents. They were greatly opposed to it but became reconciled as time went on. I had taken my ticket under my rightful name and was known from that time onwards as Warren Merriam.

One of the first pupils I taught officially as soon as I had become a certified instructor was Capt. Charles Longcroft. He would have taken his brevet sooner had it not been for an early crash in which he completely wrecked one of the school machines (Figure 19). I believe this happened on the occasion of his first solo, and he was lucky that his injuries were no more than a bad black eye and bruises. This crash, however, left us with only one instructional machine, and on this occasion Pizey did give vent to his feelings. I was in the sheds tinkering when he came in and "blew up". It was the only time I had ever seen him really roused. The fact that school work would be hindered until such time as another box-kite was obtained was certainly most exasperating, and, as Pizey would not risk any damage to his one remaining machine, instruction continued very slowly. All the pupils' nerves were at high tension at the possibility of losing their only means of flying. Such remarks as "take care, don't bust up the only one" were shouted at each pilot as he took off which, of course, only served to intensify his nervousness.

A change of instructors took place about this period. Mr. E. Hotchkiss (Figure 20) from our Salisbury school became Manager and Chief Instructor in place of Pizey, and I was appointed Assistant Instructor. Everyone was sorry when Pizey left, for he was loved by us all. As I bade him farewell, I felt I should never find another of his calibre to work with; but Hotchkiss had a charming disposition, and we pulled together well.

I had one very exciting trip as passenger with Hotchkiss on a Bristol monoplane. Apart from my initial nervousness on going solo, this was in fact the first occasion on which I experienced "cold feet". The machine being a new type to him, Hotchkiss was not at home on it. I would have given anything to have been excused the flight; but, rather than disturb our friendly relationship, I agreed with apparent cheerfulness to accompany him. It was a nerve-racking experience. Skimming the tree-tops and almost colliding with a train running along the top of the Brooklands track, we had one hair-breadth escape after another until we finally landed with a bump on the brink of the sewage farm, both feeling that we were very lucky to get down safely.

About this time I was teaching three officers who eventually took their tickets on July 6th 1912. They were Lieuts. A. Christie, H.I. Bulkeley and E.V. Anderson. The last named, with his mechanic, was killed in a mid-air collision with another R.F.C. machine piloted by Lieut. C.W. Wilson on May 12th 1914 at Farnborough. This was the first R.F.C. accident of its kind.

Wilson was descending as Anderson was climbing. Anderson and his mechanic were killed instantly, but Wilson escaped with injuries. Both machines involved were Sopwith tractor biplanes (80 h.p. Gnome).

Apart from the shortage of machines, school work was too slow. Under the system then in vogue only the most air-minded pupils were likely to get their brevets without weeks of waiting and frustration. Instruction was too vague and timid. As I was now in a position at the school to bring into practice any scheme which would improve matters, after carefully considering the risk, I started experimenting with new methods of teaching. These eventually superseded the old ones and led to much saving of time, money – and crashes. The question of time and expense was an important one. Many of the pupils were army and naval officers learning to fly from their own private resources and taking advantage of leaves to get their tuition. I think they benefited greatly from my new method, for they were generally able to learn in days as much as they had previously learned in weeks or even months. My new plan was to sit behind the pupil giving him full charge of the rudder but only part control over the joystick, until he had acquired the "feel". It was a tricky business sitting up there in the open with no straps, no protection, no instruments – and only a 50 h.p. motor, liable to peter out at any moment, to keep us airborne. I was almost entirely at the mercy of my pupil. If he got frightened and refused to do what I told him, the only control that I could reach from my position was the joystick – over his shoulder.

By living and associating very closely with the pupils outside flying hours, I was able to study their temperaments and character-istics and so get some idea of what to expect from them in the air. Each pupil required individual understanding. Some were heavy on the controls, some erratic and others impulsive; but, after mixing with them out of hours, I usually managed to sum them up pretty well. After the pupils had been given their first passenger flights I lectured them on the signs I used in the air. For movements on the rudder a squeeze on the right shoulder meant "push with the right foot", a squeeze on the left meant the same with the left foot, equal pressure on both shoulders meant "centralize rudder bar" or "straight ahead". When a pupil was sufficiently advanced to be entrusted with the joystick similar signs were employed. As I pushed his body forward or backward or to one side, he moved the joystick appropriately. The whole thing was horse sense. In fact, it often occurred to me that the use of bits and reins would be quite a sound idea. My pupils were so keen that I think that they would have even put up with these arrangements if I had suggested them. After short periods of "direct method" instruction pupils began to do wonderfully well. Soon they were able to take me for reassuring circuits, and I knew what to expect on their first solos.

There was thus no need for me to hide in the Blue Bird but, all the same, I was always relieved when first solos were over.

I think my star pupil at this period was Major John Higgins. He responded so well to the new style tuition that I was able to warm my hands in my pockets and leave him in complete control after a few short lessons. Self-confidence was essential for a pilot of those early days. I hope I will be forgiven for saying that I was self-confident and able to instil my confidence into my pupils. While confidence is still essential for a pilot, the present-day pupil has the advantage of the accumulated experience of over forty years. Though each day's flying was another step forward, we were groping about in the dark most of the time. We learned from our mistakes, but too often the penalty for a mistake was death.

Little has been written about the salaries paid to professional pilots of that period. I am not in a position to speak for any other pilot-instructor, but I don't think my own case was any exception to the general rule. My highest salary was £300 a year. On top of this I received a small commission on prizes won in competitions and on pupils introduced to the school. By modern standards my earnings were disproportionally low compared to my work and the risk I was running, but no aviator then cared much about the £.s.d. side as long as he could fly. The fascination of flying was apt to divert one's attention from its remuneration. After the First World War I was able to earn more than £1 a minute in the air for testing and experimenting with new types of aircraft and I actually earned on one occasion £50 for one flight of less than fifty minutes, but, owing to prolonged strain and previous injuries I was not able to avail myself of such favourable terms for long. For this type of job, which was very different from flying standard aeroplanes, one's nerves and health had to be in perfect condition. The present-day test pilot is, of course, even more highly paid, but the modern transport pilot also scores. His salary, according to his experience may be anything between £1,000 to £2,000 a year. He is flying machines which have been thoroughly tested and can look forward to an assured and well-paid future. It is as it should be, for a transport pilot has the lives of many people in his hands and must have considerable ability to master the ever-increasing complications of equipment and procedure.

By 1912 the *Daily Mail* had aroused much public enthusiasm and had commissioned several well-known pilots to tour the country and give flying exhibitions. Gustav Hamel, W.H. Ewen and B.C. Hucks were three who took part. Hucks wired to see if I would join them; but at that time my instructing was so all important that I refused.

By the end of July all the Salisbury pupils and school aeroplanes were transferred to Brooklands to make way for the coming military trials on the Plain. The Salisbury instructors, however, remained behind to take charge of the Company's competition machines. This change imposed a tremendous amount of extra work on the staff at Brooklands. Hotchkiss and I were continually on the go. Weather permitting, flying started at 4 a.m., and I used to rise at 3.30 a.m. and dash round the pupils' quarters to wake them – only to find that most of them, as a rule, were already up and eager to start. About this time there were twenty-four pupils at Brooklands, of whom six passed for their brevets in one week of favourable weather. All this work was accomplished with only one crash, and that only laid up the machine for a couple of days. It was afterwards acknowledged that we then created a record which eclipsed anything done previously in school work in England. I was very happy because I did not think this could have been achieved without the employment of my new teaching methods. And, perhaps owing to them, our pupils also seemed to be in a better mood for tuition.

Particularly in the summer months, air bumps made flying dangerous, and often the wind would spring up and stop every-thing. Wind was then our chief bugbear. Hour after hour would be spent watching the fluttering aerodrome flag. As soon as it stopped fluttering, out would come the aeroplanes with a rush and into them would climb the pupils. Then, just as flying was about to start, the flag would flutter again and out would climb the disgusted pupils. It was often as if the wind was ruled by some malicious imp who was determined to make fools of us and waste our time. Under these conditions we had to work such long hours that we remained in bed for a whole day during the week-end to make up our lost sleep, and the frequent absences of Hotchkiss on military duty with the Special Reserve, R.F.C., often left me single-handed.

Some of the Brooklands Aerodrome official reports of this time make interesting reading. They contain many famous names of the early days of aviation, including those of Turkish and Bulgarian officers; but Prince Cantacuzene of Romania was, I think, the first member of any royal family to learn to fly (Figure 22). He came to us from Salisbury, where he had been learning on biplanes under Harry Busteed (Figure 31). We gave him advance tuition on our monoplane and found him a very keen pupil. Reading through my album, I record the following:

> Major Brabazon coming over sewage farm had petrol pipe break, with result that he had to make hurried landing. Wheels stuck in ground, machine turned on to elevator, and threw unfortunate pilot out, but luckily with no damage, except to dignity.

Tuesday evening last week saw an abatement in weather and the Bristols came out in force. Mr. Merriam was on one biplane and Mr. Hotchkiss on another. Then both pilots started giving tuition flights to the officers – Fazil, Abdullah, Aziz, Fethi, Mehned Ali and Sahni, Captains Price and Styles, Lieuts. Glanville, Carmichael, Hope and Hanlon and Messrs. Hall, Payze and Pretyman and Lieut. Loultchiff. Messrs. Hotchkiss and Merriam were kept more than busy, as they managed to take up all these pupils a couple of times each, giving most of them a couple of circuits with a right-hand turn thrown in. In the meantime, on the two solo machines, Major Ashmore, Lieut. Joubert, Mr. Gould and Mr. Barnwell were each flying figures of eight. Messrs. Cheeseman, Summerfield, Darracq and Lieuts. Wanklyn and Playfair all flying good circuits, while Captain Boger was taxi-ing.

We could certainly claim to be busy.

Chapter 6

Some Early Crashes

August 3rd 1912 was a red letter day for the school. On this day seven of the pupils mentioned in the previous chapter obtained their brevets – R.H. Barnwell, Major the Hon. Claud Brabazon, Lieut. Shott, Lieut. P.B. Joubert de la Ferte, Major E.B. Ashmore, Lieut. C.G.S. Gould, Lieut. P.H.L. Playfair and Lieut. F.A. Wanklyn. It seemed that nothing could dampen our jubilation, but in the midst of it came the shocking news of Lindsay Campbell's crash in a field near the aerodrome (Figure 21). He was flying a Bristol monoplane and had nosedived after a stall. When Hotchkiss and I had been giving him tuition we thought he was very heavy handed on the biplanes and would not be ready to fly a monoplane for some time. At the time of the accident I was so busy that I had no idea he intended to do a circuit. He should only have been doing hops and straights. Already in his fiftieth year, Lindsay Campbell was not at a suitable age to learn to fly in those days. It was the Australian Government that had sent him to learn in order that he should be better fitted to take up an appointment as chief organizer of an Australian flying service. He had previously taken his brevet at the Salisbury School on a Bristol biplane and was having advance tuition with us when he met his death.

Hotchkiss was shortly afterwards called away on Army manoeuvres and on September 12th 1912 was himself killed on a Bristol monoplane together with his passenger. He was the first officer of the R.F.C. Reserve to meet his death while engaged on military duties.

We were all deeply affected by this accident. Gradually one or another would be taken from our midst, and we had to become hardened to the fact that in our calling nothing was certain. "Here today and gone tomorrow" was the maxim we learned to accept, but, however deeply these losses may have grieved us, the fascination of our work was too great to deter us from any further sacrifices fate might demand.

It is perhaps just as well that a life like ours also had its amusing side. The following extract is from a Report by Hotchkiss just before he was killed:

> Last Tuesday morning Mr. Percival, who was flying a Caudron biplane, was having difficulties with his machine through the Anzani engine not pulling properly. Suddenly everyone on the ground was horrified to see the machine sideslip in a ghastly manner to within a few feet of the ground. It then seemed to pick up again and continue flying. Upon landing Mr. Percival said he could not make the machine climb, and, when she started side slipping, he let go the controls and clung to the sides of the fuselage. The result was that the aeroplane, knowing a good deal about flying, corrected itself and flew straight on. This speaks very highly for the humanity of a machine that takes such great care of whoever it gives a flight to.

Caudron biplanes were used at Hendon for school work before the First World War, and, early in that war, I tried to teach pupils to fly on them; but they were quite unsuitable for instructional purposes.

In September 1912, to fill the gap caused by the death of Hotchkiss, I was appointed Manager, Chief Pilot and Instructor. Mr. W. Bendall came from Salisbury to assist me shortly after my appointment. The school was then a hive of activity, and, when the weather was too bad for flying, there were always plenty of repairs to be done in the sheds and frequent lectures to be given.

Although landings were the pupils first care and required much practice before they were smooth and well judged, they were not their major problem. The most dreaded manoeuvre was the right-hand turn. Pupils really funked doing it. Left-hand turns were easy, but, owing to the gyroscopic action of the Gnome rotary engine in flight, the nose of the aeroplane had a powerful tendency on a right-hand turn to rise into a stalling position. This was the principal peculiarity of the rotary engine-driven aircraft of those days. Given the room, it was fairly easy to make a right-hand turn, but in a limited radius it was, to say the least, very tricky. To make the turn it was necessary first to get the nose well down and then to bank and use plenty of right rudder. It was quite a difficult exercise and needed a good deal of practice and confidence. Such success as I had as an instructor in those days was attributable, I believe, to the somewhat revolutionary measures I employed. I first demonstrated the difficult exercises and then got the pupils to master them one by one before attempting the easy ones. After learning the tricky right-hand turn, for instance, they then had no difficulty in tackling the left-hand one. I found this method gave them more confidence.

Just to make life a little more exciting – as if it needed it – the rotary Gnome engine had a rather nasty habit of catching fire suddenly if you had not remembered to reduce the petrol supply before switching off for any length of time. Major Sir Alexander Bannerman was piloting a school biplane with a rotary Gnome engine one day, and had just landed, when I noticed that the engine was on fire. I rushed over, and, tearing off my coat, managed to smother the fire. It was not until the fire was out that I saw to my horror that I had been wearing my new jacket. What remained of the garment was hardly worth salvaging, but it was a relief to know that the school machine had been saved. I shall never forget the fright I had during my first night flight on a similar aeroplane. Casually glancing behind me I saw what appeared to be a gigantic "Catherine wheel". My first thought was that the engine was on fire, but I soon realized with relief that the ring of flames was caused by the exhaust gases, which were not visible in the daytime.

On September 17th six more fledglings left the nest one after the other. They were Capt. C.L. Price, Lieuts. G.B. Stopford and A.C.H. MacLean, Messrs. J.L. Hall, S. Summerfield and E.W. Cheeseman. About this time, also, the youngest certified pilot in England – fifteen-year-old midshipman N.F. Wheeler, R.N., was coming for tuition. He was a clever and plucky little pilot and obtained licence No. 370.

Competition and exhibition flying made a pleasant break from the monotony of instructional work. Under the auspices of Major Lindsay Lloyd, who worked hard to stimulate public interest in flying, several meetings were arranged by the Brooklands' Automobile Racing Club. At these meetings prizes were offered for such things as bomb dropping (with chalk bags), cross-country races, landings on a specified mark and other items. Mr. Frank Wright was the handicapper, and, among the well-known pilots who took part, were Sopwith, Spencer, Hamel, Hawker, Alcock, Sippe, Pashley, Raynham and Knight. Just as today, the crowds loved to see stunting, and all pilots would oblige with their particular "hair-raiser". The box-kites were not made for stunting, but we came very near to it with corkscrew descents and other similar manoeuvres. One show I particularly enjoyed was to stop the propeller and make a steep corkscrew descent followed by landing on a specified spot. It required considerable practice and judgement, and people always seem to think that, because the engine had stopped, a crash was inevitable. One of the first men to perform this manoeuvre was actually awarded a £500 prize. Under the heading "daring feat" I remember reading in a Southampton paper as late as 1936 the following paragraph referring to an Air Rally at Hamble:

> Flying Officer H.G. Abbott probably took the greatest risk of the afternoon by landing right in the centre of the aerodrome from a height of 1,500 feet with a stopped propeller.

So it appears that even twenty-four years later this stunt still held a thrill for the crowd.

Chapter 7

A Fruitful Year

It would occupy too much space if I were to mention all the little anecdotes and incidents with which my pupils of 1912 were concerned. I had a genuine interest in their progress and became so attached to them all that an almost brotherly affection sprung up between us which caused much worry if they met with accidents. After my pupils had passed out from the school many of them returned from time to time for joy-rides and practice. Apart from other reasons, I was always glad to have these opportunities for reassessing their skill and noting their progress. Aviation was expanding by that day, and promotion of the pupils who had left us was fast. Judged only by the number of officers and civilians who qualified at our school and were ready to go with the first squadrons on active service two years later, 1912 was a remarkably fruitful year in British aviation. The men were of the right stuff to stand the strain of their new calling and the later hazards of war, and their names bring back memories as vivid today as ever. I remember Mrs. Handasyde, wife of the designer of the Martinsyde aeroplane, was collecting autographs of all the flying men of those days and embroidering them on an afternoon teacloth – a unique idea. I wonder if that teacloth is still in existence.

One pupil of this period stands out above all the others for his delightful personality and character. Lieut. Treeby would probably never have made a brilliant pilot – he was just an average type – but, when he was killed at Salisbury through stalling a 70 h.p. Renault and diving into the ground, I felt as though part of myself had been killed with him. He seemed to me to personify the life and enthusiasm of these early fledglings, and, to this day, my own small home is named after him.

The first R.F.C. squadron of aeroplanes to be formed was No. 2, No. 1 being composed of lighter-than-air machines such as dirigibles and balloons. No. 2 began life in Farnborough but was ordered to complete its formation at what was to be its permanent base at Montrose in Scotland. On February 13th 1913, which should be a historic day in the annals of the R.F.C., five officers of No. 2 set out to fly their aeroplanes on the then almost unprecedentedly long and hazardous journey of 450 miles from Farnborough to Montrose. Three of these officers – Capt. Longcroft, Capt. Becke and Lieut. Waldron – were Brooklands' pupils who had been through my hands. In spite of very bad weather they all arrived at Montrose safely, each after experiencing difficulties in fog and being forced to land at various places on the way. It was a remarkably fine effort for those days.

Capt. Longcroft – later to become Air Vice Marshal Sir Charles Longcroft – was probably the finest pilot of the military B.E. biplane produced by the R.F.C. before the First World War. Among other noteworthy feats he made a record non-stop cross-country flight in 1913 which brought him the coveted Britannia Trophy for that year, and by 1914 his name was almost a household word in Scotland. Capt. Becke, though not so well known to the public, was little inferior to Longcroft as a pilot and was an officer much respected and admired by the R.F.C. Lieut. Waldron, who was the first of the five to reach Montrose, held the height record for the army for several months. He was only twenty-nine when he fell in action on July 3rd 1916. Soon after his arrival at Montrose he wrote me a letter in which he referred to the sad death of Geoffrey England (brother of the well-known designer, Gordon England), whose Bristol monoplane collapsed in mid-air.

While on the subject of the early R.F.C. pilots I am reminded of Lieut. P.J. Joubert de la Ferte who was a first-class pupil. He later rose to very high rank and is probably well known to many radio listeners of the present generation for his admirable talks on the radio during the last war and the pleasant quality of his voice. While running my aviation bureau in London in 1928 I had occasion to write to the then Air Marshal Joubert de la Ferte and was more than amused at this concluding remark in his reply:

Your telegraphic address *"exboxkite"* recalls visions of the sewage farm at 50 feet.

He still remembered one of Brooklands' outstanding characteristics.

Major J.F.A. Higgins, R.A., later achieved distinction and rose to high rank in the R.A.F. He had served in the South African War of 1899-1902, and no doubt his previous experience of active service was largely responsible for his being such a wonderfully apt pupil. At one time there were two Major Higgins in the R.F.C. Our Major J.F.A., being notable for his rather prominent posterior and a monocle, was invariably referred to throughout his distinguished career by the old hands in the R.F.C. and R.A.F. as "bum and eyeglass" – an appellation about which I am sure he always knew and never resented.

Another memorable pupil was Lieut. Read. His service in the air was lamentably short lived. Though he had shewn great promise, it was later discovered that his eyesight was not up to the required standard for flying. He therefore returned to his old regiment and was killed in an action for which he received the posthumous award of the Victoria Cross.

Some mastered the art of flying more quickly than others. Sidney Pickles, for instance, was the quickest and most adaptable pupil I trained during this period. To him flying was second nature. He was over-confident at times, but that was his only fault and did not prevent him from speedily joining the front row of our best pre-war test pilots. Others needed much coaxing and patience, and yet the slow ones turned out the steadiest in the long run.

R.H. Barnwell had almost despaired of becoming a pilot. He was slow in his movements at the controls and inclined to be heavy handed. At one stage he became so depressed that he asked me to tell him candidly whether I thought he would ever turn out to be any good. Encouragement and patience, however, resulted in a much coveted brevet, and I never regretted the time and care I had given him. Soon after getting his certificate he became Chief Pilot Instructor to Vickers, where he did excellent work as instructor and test pilot.

One more pupil to get his ticket at the end of this year deserves mention – Capt. D.W. Powell. He was peculiarly reluctant to fly solo, even when quite capable of doing so, and I flew as his passenger for a good while before I could convince him he should go alone. When he eventually made his first circuit alone he was so pleased and confident that he asked to be allowed to take his brevet test straight away. While he did it, everyone remarked how well he flew, little realizing that he had made many circuits before with me sitting like a dummy in the back seat. To sit alone in a pilot's seat of a box-kite at 1,000 feet or more presented to some pupils an uncanny feeling of loneliness or emptiness. Capt. Powell never told me of his apprehensions in this respect, but I instinctively detected them in him, as I did in others. Many pupils, I found, were glad when they could enjoy the protection of the partially closed-in cockpit of the tractor planes. I have often wondered what the pilot of today would feel like in a box-kite and how he would react.

It was on Christmas Day 1912 that Santa Claus made his first official flight in a British plane. Sponsored by Colonel Lindsay Lloyd and dressed as Father Christmas, I was staged to fly a Bristol biplane to Brooklands loaded with parcels for a large crowd of children. There I was greeted with shrill cries of delight as I circled the aerodrome with my beard and whiskers flapping in the breeze and landed right in front of them (Figure 23). There were nearly 400 children waiting for presents. During the next few days I was bombarded with letters of thanks from many of the children or their parents. Writing about children reminds me that my small daughter Winifred first flew with me in 1912. She was then only six and had to sit on the knees of one of my pupils. She revelled in the flight and was, I believe, the first small child ever to fly in Britain.

To sum up the work of our school, which headed the list for pupils trained in the year 1912 – out of a total of 211 for the whole country we trained 98 at Brooklands and Salisbury Plain. Just how great our effort was can be seen by the fact that the highest total of any other school was 20. Mr. R. Dallas Brett comments as follows in his *History of British Aviation, 1908-14*:

> The Bristol Company's effort was truly prodigious. Their gross output of pilots was almost two per week. Few of the flying clubs of the present day could equal the output of the Brooklands' Branch of the Bristol's, in spite of the accumulated knowledge and improved equipment of twenty years.

Chapter 8

Never a Dull Moment

In spite of wintry weather and open machines, 1913 started with a busy round of tuition. Sunday afternoons were set aside for visitors, and pupils usually brought their friends. Those who were sufficiently advanced would be allowed to display their capabilities in handling the box-kite before admiring relatives. All pilots had their fans, and it was encouraging to see the growing enthusiasm of the public at that early date. Many distinguished people came for joy rides to test the thrills of the new sport. Lieut.-Col. Sykes, the Commander of the military wing R.F.C. and the ninety-fifth certified pilot in this country, would either send or bring his friends for me to take up. His enthusiasm and confidence in aviation and his practical foresight was shown by the fact that most of the friends he brought were young men. C.R. Fairey, the well-known designer and constructor, was my passenger when I went to test Bristol machines for the newly formed R.N.A.S. at Eastchurch. I believe it was his first flight, and he was able, with his long arms, to reach over my shoulder and follow my movements on the joystick. Fairey was then with the Short Brothers, Horace, Eustace and Oswald. Major the Hon. C.W. Lowther, son of the Speaker of the House of Commons, Lord Ullswater, also flew with me about this time. He was most anxious to learn to fly. C.C. Turner, the pioneer aviator and the first journalist to obtain his brevet, frequently flew with me as passenger. Last of all, but by no means least, was Jack Alcock, who was knighted in 1919 for being the first to fly the Atlantic. He also took friendly tuition from me at this time and occasionally accompanied me when I was testing.

Wives, mothers and sweethearts of my pupils, all were taken up – and so were my lady friends. I have good reason to remember one lady passenger. I will not divulge her name, but, should she read these lines, she may feel consolation in the fact that a similar experience – though of a more disconcerting nature – befell me later on with one of my war pupils. At her request I had to climb to well over 1,000 feet so that she could have the thrill of a prolonged spiral descent. When above the aerodrome I switched off the engine and stuck the nose of the machine down. The dropping sensation must have been too much for my fair companion. The next moment her arms were entwined tightly round my neck and she was screaming, "take me down; take me down". For some time I could not reach the engine switches and was almost strangled by her grip before I could land. It must seem strange to pilots of today that we carried passengers in open machines and that none of us were strapped in.

Spiral descents were always an attraction for the visitors and passengers, but the steeper corkscrew descents in which I specialized were more spectacular. These, however, could not be carried out with passengers because of the danger of them falling on the pilot, or, worse still, becoming giddy and falling right out of the machine. These and other antics on early aircraft earned me the title of "Box-Kite King". Will there ever be anything quite as exhilarating as those open machines, with the wind whistling round and playing weird music on the struts and wires and the shouted conversations? Quaint, "stick and string", they might have been, but I cannot help feeling that much of the joy of flying is lost to the modern pilot shut up in the cabin of his aeroplane. Being out in the open, we seemed to acquire a sense of balance quite unknown to the pilots who learned to fly on the later aircraft. Without instruments, for they were then practically unknown, we learned to fly with an accuracy that became almost instinctive. I still think insufficient attention is paid in elementary instruction to flying without the aid of instruments. A pupil should learn by "feel", and, only when he can acquire this "feel", should he be allowed to make use of instrumental aids.

It was in 1913 that I was given a commission as Lieutenant in the Legion of Frontiersmen. One day Colonel Driscoll, our Commandant, came up with me as a passenger to spot some of his mounted troopers who were supposed to be hiding from air observation. Much to their surprise, we spotted them in the vicinity of Byfleet and dropped a message to say so. Colonel Driscoll's son, incidentally, came under my instruction at the beginning of the First World War. I was always nervous of flying as a passenger with any but my own pupils. I did, however, stretch a point with Tom Sopwith on one of his new biplanes and also with M. Jullerot (Figure 26). They were both very cool headed and reliable pilots. I was to have flown with Graham Gilmore on his fatal flight, but was too busy to leave when the time came for his take-off. I helped him to get away and shortly afterwards received a telephone message to say that he had been killed in a crash at Richmond Park.

A mid-air crash always had a peculiar terror for me, and I think this fear was shared by most contemporary aviators. One day when up with a pupil I had a queer experience which temporarily took the stuffing out of me. It was a day when a lot of loose clouds were floating about, and we were nipping in and out of them. On coming out of one, the sun cast a mirror-like shadow of our machine on the cloud in front of us. So realistic was this shadow that I was convinced we were on the point of colliding with another aircraft, and, without giving myself time to think, I dived sharply to avoid the crash.

M. Pégoud, the French aviator who was the first man to loop the loop, demonstrated before an enormous crowd of spectators at Brooklands about this time. To us aviators the scientific aspect of looping and upside-down flying was even more impressive than the spectacular. Pégoud showed us that, given sufficient height, we could rectify a spin or any other untoward situation, provided that the aircraft did not break up in the air. Before seeking to emulate him we set about adjusting and strengthening our machines to bear the extra strain. These demonstrations gave us more confidence, and the stunting was later to become invaluable to pilots in air combat.

When school work one day was cancelled because of weather conditions, I took a pupil named Pendlebury in a box-kite to visit the St. Nicholas Home for Crippled Children, near Byfleet. We arrived over the village at about 3,000 feet and, to quote the newspaper, "made a magnificent spiral descent to the unbounded delight of the children who had been looking forward to the promised visit with so much interest". The joy of the children certainly compensated me for the difficulty I had in getting away again. Owing to the many obstacles in the restricted area I decided on subsequent visits to make the journey by road; but to the children, I was always the "wonder man from the sky", and their enthusiasm made a lasting impression on my mind.

Gusts of wind and bumps were things to be feared by box-kite pilots. Coming in to land one Sunday afternoon at Brooklands – a day when I should really not have been flying because of the wind – a terrific gust beat my machine down to five or six feet from the ground. I bounced off my seat, hit my head against the top of the plane and then rebounded on to my seat like a rubber ball. To everyone's relief and astonishment, I managed to grab the controls and effect a safe landing. Shortly afterwards, Gustav Hamel murmured confidently as he followed me into the hangar that if I courted trouble in this way he would soon be subscribing towards another wreath. Coming from a man like Hamel, notoriously indifferent to his own safety, this was almost laughable. How often had I been forced to speak to him about neglecting his machine and to tell my mechanic to adjust and mend parts to prevent it breaking up in the air.

About this time I was credited with a romance that was actually Hamel's. It so happened that he had made a "date" with a lady friend at Chertsey. Knowing that I was well acquainted with landing grounds in that vicinity, he asked me to fly ahead and show him where to land. This I did, and, being first to land, was the first to be greeted by the lady, who, in her excitement, took my muffled figure to be Hamel's. When the papers appeared the next day with headlines – "A dashing young aviator", "Love in the Air" – it was I who first received the teasing and congratulations.

With about fifty pupils gaining their brevets between January and September 1913, Bendall and I were kept so busy that we had no time for even a week-end off, let alone a summer holiday. We were pleased with the results of our work and were too occupied to notice that our success was causing some jealousy in other quarters. Evidence of this came home to me in an unexpected and forcible manner when, in returning from an instructional flight, I was way-laid at the doorway of my office and given a hefty punch on the jaw by a former flying colleague. On hearing of this incident, about half a dozen of my pupils bundled me into the school lorry and drove me to my assailant's home, where they demanded an apology. As it turned out, we had no difficulty in getting this, accompanied with the excuse that the offender was a "bit tight" at the time. It is pleasant

1. The Author as a Flight Lieutenant in the Royal Naval Air Service, Chingford, 1915.

2.   Banking a Bristol Box-kite over Brooklands Aerodrome in 1912.

3. Sir Winston Churchill inspecting a Short No. 2 "School Machine", 1912.

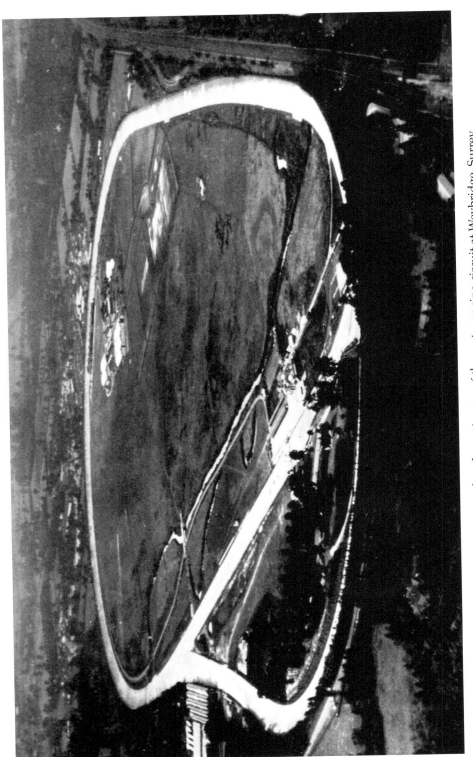

4. An aerial view of Brooklands Aerodrome within the perimeter of the motor-racing circuit at Weybridge, Surrey.

5. Ballooning at East Horndon, Essex, in 1907; Oswald Short and the Hon. Claud Brabazon in the hoop, and Griffith Brewer and Eustace Short in the basket.

6. Captain Sir Geoffrey de Havilland in one of the machines of his own design in which he taught himself to fly.

7. J.T.C. Moore-Brabazon (later Lord Brabazon of Tara) in his Voisin biplane, "Bird of Passage", 1908.

8. Sir Alliott Verdon Roe in his triplane at Lea Marshes in 1909. He landed in the river Lea which runs past the houses in the photograph.

9. An Avro 504B, designed for Sir A. Verdon Roe, with an 80 h.p. Gnome engine.

10. The original Blackburn monoplane, 1909. It crashed on its first flight.

11. Colonel S.F. Cody at Brooklands in 1912.

12. Sir Thomas Sopwith in an early Howard-Wright biplane.

13. Sir Frederick Handley Page in April 1910 in *Bluebird,* his first aeroplane, built in 1909.

14. Grahame-White's Henry Farman "pusher" seaplane at a seaside resort during his "Wake up England" tour for the *Daily Mail*, 1912.

15. Claude Grahame-White, 1910.

16. Collyns Pizey, in the pilot's seat of a Bristol biplane, with some of the 1911 pupils at Brooklands.

17. The Author flying his first "straight" at Brooklands in 1911.

18. The author with Harold Barnwell, sitting behind, in a 1910 Bristol biplane. "First bulldog to fly, 1912. Harold Barnwell holding the dog while I piloted. It is generally known that once a bulldog digs his teeth into one it doesn't let go … this was in my mind and although rather restless at first he soon got used to the sensation and seemed to enjoy his novel experience."

19. Captain Charles Longcroft's crash on his first solo flight in 1912.

20. Edward Hotchkiss seated in a Bristol biplane at Larkhill, Salisbury, 1912.

21. Showing the wreckage to Lindsay Campbell's widow at her request, Brooklands, 1912.

22. Prince Cantacuzene of Romania swinging the propeller of a Bristol monoplane.

23. Santa Claus arrives by Box-kite, Christmas, 1912.

24. "The old School Bus", 1912: (*left to right*) Lt. The Hon. John D. Boyle, the Author, Captain R. Pigot, W. Bendall (Assistant Instructor), Major A.B. Forman, Lt. John Empson, Lt. R. Kitson, and Lt. R.M. Rodwell.

to remember that one of those who accompanied me on this errand was Lieut. Frank Beevor, a pupil of a rival school.

I next noticed that a number of pupils from other schools were hanging around our shed and soon learnt that some were determined to transfer to us. The reason for our success was fairly obvious. I was then the only instructor at Brooklands who was prepared to take the risk of sitting behind pupils and allowing them full control of the machine in the air. My old friend and pupil, Barnwell, was Chief Instructor to the Vickers School and had been taught to fly this way, but even he would not at first adopt this method when he became an instructor. It was clear that unless the other instructors were prepared to take the risk they might as well pack up. After a few friendly discussions, Barnwell and his assistant, Knight, eventually came to this conclusion, and, in due course, the Vickers School began to flourish. Among their pupils who became famous in later years were Major W. Sefton Brancker, Capts. Hugh C. Dowding, W.G.H. Salmond, L.E.O. Charlton, Lieut. W.G.S. Mitchell, Mr. R.K. Pierson (Vickers' designer) and Mr. J. Lankester Parker.

Both R.H. Barnwell and his brother, Capt. F.S. Barnwell (Chief Designer to the Bristol Aeroplane Company), were early pioneers in building aircraft. The former was really never cut out for instructional work, but he excelled at testing experimental machines and did much of this highly dangerous work. Early in the First World War he flew to see me at Chingford and was killed while flying a day or so afterwards. There were few, indeed, who did care for the task of instructing. I still feel that instructing is a natural gift and that instructors can never be made. A good pilot is not necessarily a good instructor, but a good instructor must first be a good pilot. Apart from a great liking for the work and other qualities, a good instructor must be difficult to ruffle, have untiring patience and be something of a psychologist. Too many of the few instructors of this period varied between the exigent, the over-critical, the hasty, the apathetic and the over-anxious. I myself was deeply fond of flying and often wished I could break away from the constant drudgery of school work. I should have liked to have taken up experimental flying, but something always seemed to hold me to instructing.

One day, after several hours of strenuous morning tuition, I had returned to my digs to get some much needed sleep. The weather had changed for the worse, and, before going to my room, I had instructed my landlady that I was not to be disturbed on any account. I had just fallen asleep when someone banged on my door, and, despite the protests of my landlady came bouncing in. It was Pemberton-Billing. "What the devil do you mean by coming in here?" I demanded. Apologizing profusely for his rude intrusion, Pemberton-Billing explained that he had to get his brevet in a day to win a bet of £500 made with Mr. Handley Page, "And", he said, "you are the only man who can help me to win it." This explanation put a different complexion on matters. Forgetting my fatigue and annoyance, I dressed and in half an hour was telephoning my headquarters for their consent. The Secretary, Mr. Henry White-Smith, said it could not be done. "Apart from the stupidity of this idea" he testily retorted, "don't you realize you are asking for a crash and consequent delay in school work?" Not daunted by this reply I took Pemberton-Billing along with me to the Vickers School and introduced him to Barnwell. But his firm also refused to take the responsibility. However, someone having produced an old Henry Farman box-kite, Barnwell took the risk of giving Pemberton-Billing intensive private tuition, with the result that "P.B." did qualify for his brevet in a day and won his bet. It was a terrifying ordeal. We who were watching held our breath at the hair-raising behaviour of his machine as it stalled badly on every right-hand turn and performed other amazing and unrehearsed feats. It was a wager pluckily won, and the greatest possible credit should be given to Barnwell for the risk he took in sitting in the passenger seat when giving "P.B." tuition. He adhered more or less to my system of instruction. Had he not done so, I do not think that "P.B." could ever have succeeded. He and I were to meet again in the second year of the war, when he was a Flight Commander, R.N., and came to me for advanced instruction on Avro biplanes.

Chapter 9

The Price of Knowledge

My first flight in brilliant moonlight occurred one evening when I was returning from the skating rink at Woking with a number of pupils on the school lorry. Struck by the stillness of the air and visibility, we trundled a box-kite out of a hangar. I did not think then that it would be advisable to give the pupils a lesson in this light, but they all enjoyed the novelty of flying by moonlight sitting in the passenger seat. Though I had never before taken off in moonlight, I had once landed. It was late one evening after school work when I had taken my fiancée – now my wife – for a trip on which we flew around until long after sunset.

One of the most tragic fatalities of this period concerned a former pupil of mine. Major J.C. Merrick was really too old to learn to fly and had been a very difficult and slow pupil, but, as he was a brave and persevering man, I eventually got him through his brevet test. About five months later he was killed at the Central Flying School, Upavon, while making a steep glide into the aerodrome. He was flying a Short biplane and must have slipped out of his seat and, falling forward on to the joystick, caused a vertical dive which threw him out. Of course he was killed instantly, and the tragedy was deepened by the knowledge that, had he been strapped in, the accident would never have happened. It must seem curious to the modern pilot that we were so long in realizing the importance of straps.

Lord Edward Grosvenor took his brevet on August 29th 1913. Quite one of the heaviest of pupils, he was also one of the quickest; and he did much to foster aviation before and after the war. It was not long before he took his place among our leading sporting pilots, and he was actually the fourth British pilot to loop the loop. As a memento of this occasion, he gave me one of the first aeroplane altimeters reading to 6,000 feet and made by Callaghan & Co., London. Mr. R.R. Skene, another brilliant pupil at that time, was the next to follow suit in this great stunt of the day. Like Lord Edward Grosvenor, he looped on a Blériot monoplane. The distinction of being the first passenger to loop belongs to Mr. Vernon Jones, then on the staff of *Flight*. He did it with Monsieur Louis Noel at Hendon.

A few words about a young friend, L.F. McDonald, who was the first pupil of the Bristol Flying School to get his ticket in 1910. It was No. 28. When we met, he was Assistant Pilot at Vickers to Capt. H.F. Wood, who was the fourth pilot at our school to qualify (No. 37). At the time McDonald met his death he was testing a Vickers Tractor plane at Erith. It appeared that his engine had been giving trouble before he took off. While still at a low altitude the machine began to lose height, and he tried to turn back to the aerodrome. He failed to reach it, and his aeroplane came down in the Thames, in which both he and his mechanic, Mr. H. England, were drowned. It seemed sad that it should have been mainly through accidents like these that we had to learn the rights and wrongs of flying. Each accident served to warn others, but it sometimes seemed that the price we had to pay was tragically high.

Another personal blow was the death of Lieut. J. Crawford-Kehrmann who was, I believe, the first officer in the Royal Flying Corps to be killed in action while flying in France. I remember so well taking a snapshot of him in a group with his mother and sister. He and I had a narrow escape one morning when we collided with the Pashley Brothers' machine in a mist. Unknown to me, Pashley had landed at one end of the aerodrome. As he was turning round on the ground, our machine came in to land and collided with him. Luckily no one was hurt, but our box-kite was almost overturned by the impact and the gauge glass nearest to Pashley's head was knocked clean off. The Pashleys took the case to court and won it. Since neither judge nor counsel knew much about flying, it was a novel case for the courts and attracted much interest. The view was taken that it was imprudent on my part to allow a pupil to have full control of the machine.

But I must not stress the sombre side of flying too much, for there were many humorous incidents. One occurred when we were offered £5 by a certain Institute, meeting in London, to stage an Aircraft Display. Though we thought the sum an insult, we decided to accept the offer. When the Institute members arrived full of expectation they were faced with an exhibition of every bit of old aircraft wreckage we could find on the aerodrome. Not unnaturally, our visitors were surprised and annoyed to find that we were making fun of them, but we relented and gave them a show without accepting any payment.

I shall always remember what a stir it created when the rumour reached us that suffragettes intended to storm our hangars at midnight. The knowledge of their amazingly destructive powers was not comforting, and a number of the aerodrome staff decided to lie in wait to try and catch them red-handed. As the general idea was to remove their outer clothes and chase them off the aerodrome in their "undies", it was, perhaps, just as well that the rumour proved to be unfounded.

No little excitement was caused one day at Brooklands when for the first and, I believe, the only time on any English aerodrome, a monoplane, balloon, biplane, dirigible and spherical balloon were seen in the air together. Harold Barnwell was flying a Vickers monoplane; the new "Beta" dirigible from Aldershot was making a circuit of the aerodrome; Mr. James Radley and Lieut. Waterlow, R.N., arrived at the same time in a Short balloon from Battersea, and I amused myself by flying circuits round the balloon and dirigible in a Bristol box-kite. The balloonists landed for tea and then took off, landing a second time at Witney. This was the first balloon to land at Brooklands, although many previous attempts had been made. Shortly afterwards, a German "Parsival" airship, ordered by the British Admiralty for the R.N.A.S., flew over Brooklands and London from Farnborough on its first flight in this country. Among the passengers on this occasion were Capt. F. Murray Sueter, R.N., the first Director of the R.N.A.S., and Lieut. F.L.M. Boothby, R.N. The airship was piloted by Major Stelling, assisted by Herr Schaak and two German mechanics. It attracted a great deal of attention on account of the rumours which were circulating at that time about mysterious visits by German airships over England. In this year, C.C. Turner made a three-hour ascent in a "Mammoth" accompanied by twelve journalists, among whom was Bennett Burleigh, the famous war correspondent. The pilot aeronaut on this occasion was A.E. Gaudron. Incidentally, Oswald Short can now claim to be the earliest balloon pilot still living. He made his first balloon ascent with his brother Eustace in 1898. I must confess that ballooning did not appeal to me. I found that there was no "sensation" in the flight of a balloon. Judging by the number who later switched over to aeroplanes, such as Short, F.K. McClean, Maitland and Turner, many balloonists must, I think, have felt the same way. Harold Piffard, for instance, who died shortly before the Second World War, started ballooning in 1904 and experimented with a number of his own models. But he too gave up ballooning and finally built a heavier-than-air machine on the lines of the Wright, Cody and Curtiss biplanes.

It was later in 1913 that S. Corbett-Wilson, then airship test pilot at the Royal Aircraft Factory, carried out the first known air tow. The R.N. Airship "Willows" was marooned at Odiham with a damaged engine, and Lieut-Commander Usborne, the officer-in-charge, was proposing to tow it back to Farnborough by hand. Corbett-Wilson suggested that it might be towed by another airship, and, after consultation with the O.C. No. 1 Airship Wing, the ETA, under command of Major Waterlow, was sent from Farnborough with Corbett-Wilson aboard. Using a 600-feet tow rope weighted in the middle with a ballast bag to stop it fouling the rudders and elevators of the "Willows", the ETA made the tow successfully against a 10 m.p.h. wind at a ground speed of 10 m.p.h.

Soon after the airship and the balloon episode, one of the best-known and most courageous of Australian aeronauts and a man who had toured Australia making numerous thrilling descents over land and sea – once he had to dodge sharks in Sydney Harbour, came to England to learn to fly heavier-than-air machines. When he flew with me, I did not think he had the makings of a pilot, and, finding him almost stone deaf, I did not press him to continue. When he left he wrote to me saying that he believed he would be a flyer yet – "If not a star, at least a twinkler." He must have had many near escapes during his career, for he told me he had broken almost every bone in his body at one time or another.

When I go through letters from old pupils I can live through those days again as though they were the happenings of only yesterday. The sincere words of gratitude and the many little keepsakes are very pleasant reminders of the group of grand fellows to whom it was my good fortune to impart knowledge and experience. Still cherished among my souvenirs is a now broken spirit flask presented to me by Lieuts. R.E. Pierse and T.W. Mulchay-Morgan – "for the amount of trouble you have taken teaching the antics of a box-kite". I took the flask with me on many of my cross-country flights and war-time patrols, and during one of them I dropped it and smashed the glass. Another memento I prize very much is a gold match-box bearing the signature of L.H. Strain, K.C. He was a very keen and popular pupil. Like the flask, it has been through the wars but is always a happy reminder. Some of these mementos bring back sad memories. Capt. W. Picton-Warlow sent me a wrist-watch to commemorate his successful brevet test in 1913. It was while I was wearing it that I heard the news that he had disappeared in the Channel on a flight back from France. By a strange coincidence I was still wearing that watch when I narrowly escaped drowning myself a few years later.

Cross-country flights were becoming increasingly popular in 1913, and it was a welcome change to have pilots from other schools coming over to see us. Some would come to visit their old instructors and friends; others came with machines which they demonstrated and hoped to sell. Geoffrey de Havilland, Cody, H. Busteed, and B.C. Hucks were just a few of the names of our distinguished visitors recorded at that time. But these flights were carried out with no small factor of risk and rarely without incident. One never felt safe or comfortable about one's departed visitors until telephone calls came through to say that they had arrived safely.

In August 1913, W. Bendall, who had been assisting me so admirably with school work for about twelve months, unfortunately had to give up flying because of nerve strain after an accident. He did so not without a struggle, and some tears, and I, too, was most affected. We had always been in perfect harmony, and he had done splendid work for aviation.

Until the appointment of Mr. R.R. Skene, a former pupil, as Assistant Instructor, I had to work on my own, but nevertheless managed in a single week to get seven pupils through their brevet tests. Among them were Capts. H.C. Jackson and L.P. Evans of the Staff College and Lieut. C.C. Darley. Darley passed his test brilliantly, rising steadily to 2,000 feet – at that time a record for a pupil – and effected a landing close to the mark after a well-executed spiral descent. There was keen competition among the pupils for the height record, and when Darley, leaving Brooklands the following day, heard that Richard Powell was out to break his record he wired him: "If you break my record, I'll come back and break your neck." But Powell did break his record, by 250 feet, and both he and Darley still live to tell the tale.

The mention of this trio of names – Skene, Darley and Powell – reminds me that Powell was not long at Brooklands before he discovered that there was some sport to be had with the rabbits which infested the banking outside the track and came out after dusk to feed on the green grass of the aerodrome. His plan was to drive slowly round the track in his car (a 15·9 1913 Sporting Sunbeam) with the head-lamps on. Skene, Darley and Lord Edward Grosvenor joined him many times in this entertainment. Powell always drove while his friends took turns with the gun, which was provided by Skene. The man with the gun always sat in the back seat, so as to give him a good view over the front of the car with the windscreen down. Keeping a running rabbit in the beam of the head-lights was sufficiently difficult to be exciting, and they often found themselves near the top of the banking. Darley was by far the best shot and rarely missed.

One night these four sportsmen had been amusing themselves in this way, and, after putting the car away in the Bristol shed, went across to the Blue Bird Restaurant for drinks. That night there were a number of people dining there, and when my friends entered the dining-room Grosvenor was carrying the gun. It so happened that, hanging from one of the roof girders, was a champagne bottle which had been placed there by some revellers in the past. No sooner did they enter the restaurant when Grosvenor let drive at the bottle, which he hit but did not break. Before anybody had a chance to stop him, he slipped in another cartridge and fired again. This time he smashed the bottle into such small fragments that broken glass and small shot were flying all over the place. I had never seen anything off the films like the scene that followed. Women in full evening dress were screaming, falling down and crawling underneath the tables; men were running about shouting and swearing; complete pandemonium reigned.

Fortunately no serious consequences ensued; but next day Mrs. Billing utterly refused to serve Powell and Darley with coffee and ordered them out. This was most upsetting and very inconvenient. Something had to be done to put things straight. The next night, Powell, Darley and Skene went out on a really serious rabbit hunt. They drove round and round the track until they had bagged no less than nine rabbits, which they then bore in a body to the Blue Bird and laid them, so to speak, at Mrs. Billing's feet. With the rabbits they also offered a very complete apology. Mrs. Billing tried to maintain her uncompromising attitude, but the row of rabbits was too much for her, and, after going into fits of laughter, she once more made them free of her establishment.

Skene, one of the first to be killed in France in the early days of the First World War, was not favourably impressed with school work. By temperament he was a test pilot and later left the school to become one of Britain's foremost test pilots. He was succeeded by F.B. Halford, later to achieve fame as an aero-engine designer. Able assistant though he was, Halford, too, could not settle down to instructing. His aim was to get on to the experimental side of the Royal Aircraft Factory at Farnborough. Though I regretted losing him, I was able to help him to achieve this aim. He started work immediately on B.E. army aeroplanes, in a later model of which Lieut. Robinson brought down the first Zeppelin. Two Brooklands' incidents of Halford's time are worth recounting. In the first, one of his pupils, then suffering with "D.Ts", had an attack in the air and insisted on doing the opposite to everything he was told to do. Halford, sitting in the back with no controls, was almost at his wits end. Luckily, he had the presence of mind to think out the reverse of his true instructions and then shout them to the pupil. In this way they eventually got down safely. We did manage to get this pupil solo, but his first flight was like a scenic railway trip. The other incident occurred when the same pupil bought a Caudron biplane before he could fly properly and set off on a cross-country flight to visit a lady friend. He tried to land in her garden, found it was too small, and crashed while trying to climb out with his engine still switched off. To those of us sitting in the Blue Bird doubtfully awaiting his return the news of his crash did not come as a surprise.

In addition to my work as Pilot Instructor I had the management of the business to attend to, a log of all lessons and flights to make up, and the progress of each pupil to report every day to headquarters. Machines had to be overhauled and inspected, and it was surprising what a lot of small damage they sustained in the course of tuition work. It was lucky, therefore, that I had loyal and good workers in my clerk, Mr. Cork, and chief mechanic, Mr. Willis, both of whom helped to make the school such a success. And I must not forget Whisky, the Irish terrier who was everybody's pet. He used to wait patiently for his joy rides and was as fond of the pilots and mechanics as they were of him.

When the work of the School started to slacken down in October 1913, I asked to be allowed to go to Salisbury Plain for experiments on the newer types of aircraft. The firm were agreeable, and, although it was rather a wrench, I soon found I was almost back on home ground. The Salisbury Plain pupils were so keen to have instruction that I had to fit in my flights on the new aircraft between long periods of instructional flying. M. Jullerot (Figure 26), Manager and Chief Instructor at Larkhill, and Herr Willy Voigt, one of his former pupils, were glad of my assistance and even took advanced tuition under me on the monoplanes. Jullerot became a Major in the R.F.C. during the war.

Salisbury Plain impressed me with its unlimited space for landing – so unlike Brooklands with its sewage farm, railings, railway line, trees and scattered hangars. There, it was easier to learn to fly, but, on that account, I favoured Brooklands as an instructional centre. Pupils on the Plain had no worry about obstacles and did not, in my opinion, develop such a fine sense of judgement, as the Brooklands pupils. It was while on the Plain that I flew over to see some of my previous pupils, who were now at the Central Flying School, Upavon. I made a trip with Lieut. J.D. Harvey, R.N., and we were accorded a warm reception by the Commandant, Capt. Godfrey Paine, R.N., and his second-in-command, Major H.M. Trenchard. Leaving rather late, we flew into a thick mist on the way back which obscured all landmarks. After circling for a while we made a landing almost in darkness at Newton Tony and there secured the machine for the night. When I returned the following morning with my passenger to collect the machine I had a nasty shock. It was only a few yards from a precipice. Had we rolled a little farther on landing, we should both have been killed.

Some of the monoplanes were veritable death-traps and should never have been used as instructional aircraft. Although I don't think the fault was always to be found in their construction – much could be said about the inexperience of their pilots – yet on several occasions these machines actually broke up while flying. A Bristol monoplane which broke up in the air was responsible for the death of Hotchkiss, and Geoffrey England met his death in the same manner.

Though my stay at Salisbury was brief, I gained the experience I needed and returned to Brooklands, once more ready for the fray. The year was drawing to its close. Among the last pupils were Capt. H.E. Walcott, Sub-Lieut. C.R. Bromet, R.N., and Lieut. E.D. Maxwell Robertson, R.N. The last named worked at the Admiralty, lived at Weybridge, and had to fit his lessons in during the evenings. Bromet served in the Dardanelles and France in the First World War, eventually transferring to the R.A.F. and being promoted to Air Commodore. So many of the naval and army officers who had spent their spare time and money in learning to fly found it was not easy to transfer at once into the small Flying Corps, which had only just been formed. I was happy to find that most of the pupils whom I recommended personally were soon successful.

When we came to reckon up the pupils trained during 1913 we found we had beaten all records. Even the achievements of 1912, great as they seemed, were dwarfed. Between them, the Brooklands and Salisbury schools had trained 117 pupils: (Brooklands, 70), and the only other civil schools in the running were Vickers (35), Ewen (25) and Grahame-White (19). As Mr. R. Dallas Brett again comments in his *History of British Aviation, 1908-14*:

> The Bristol School had now reached its peak. Mr. Warren Merriam, M.H. Jullerot and their able assistants deserve the very highest praise. Between them they had trained only nine short of the total number of pupils who had qualified at all the other sixteen civilian schools put together. It was phenomenal.

I was tremendously pleased, and, had it not been for one thing, there would have been no happier man. Alas! I had failed to pass my eyesight test for the R.N.A.S. Reserve.

Chapter 10

My First Bad Crash

January 1st 1914, saw the dawning of a happy new year for at least one person. Sub-Lieut. F.G. Saunders, R.N.V.R., obtained his brevet under the new rules of the Royal Aero Club after two-and-three-quarter hours' instruction, all on the same day. A couple of weeks later a merry trio followed suit. They were Lieut. J.T. Cull, R.N., Sub-Lieut. J.R.W. Smyth-Pigott, R.N., and Lieut. H.E.M. Watkins, R.N.R. To celebrate their success they presented the official observer with a banana in which they had inserted three golden sovereigns. Just as he was about to take a large bite, Watkins called out, "Be careful", and it was just as well, because the piece he would have bitten off had a sovereign in it.

As things became fairly quiet at the school after these three sailors had departed, I took the opportunity of visiting Salisbury Plain for more practice.

It was while flying on the Plain this time in a dual-control side-by-side machine we called the "Sociable" that I met with my first serious crash (Figure 29). Unfortunately my passenger was killed, while I merely sustained a broken jaw and other injuries.

Fitted with a 50 h.p. Gnome, the "Sociable" was underpowered, but it seemed to be flying quite normally until, as we were about to go into a left-hand turn, I noticed that my passenger, Lancelot Gipps, was rigid on the rudder. I struggled with the rudder-bar and shouted to him to relax, but he appeared not to hear me and took no notice. Then, without warning, he suddenly released control, thus causing me to rudder violently. The plane nose-dived sickeningly and started to crash before I had a chance to recover. Luckily, I had the presence of mind to switch off before we hit the ground and so prevent a fire. Lieut. Griffin, who saw the crash, said that I staggered from the machine and collapsed, but Gipps only lived a few minutes. As I was in a pretty bad state myself I was not told about Gipps' death until I had recovered. A very clever operation was performed on my jaw at the Bristol Royal Infirmary by Dr. T. Carwardine.

I have often been asked to describe what my feelings were when I knew that the crash was inevitable. My mind was so occupied in switching-off the ignition and petrol to avoid fire that I had no time to think of anything else. At the inquiry the Royal Aero Club Accidents Committee were of the opinion that the accident was due to ruddering violently when the aircraft was unbanked through the pupil first resisting the control and then suddenly yielding. They recommended that in all dual-control machines used for instructing, means should be provided whereby the instructor could instantly disconnect the pupil's controls.

In six weeks I was back on flying. There were no medical restrictions or rules to say when we were fit, although Dr. Allen Hope, of Adlestone, occasionally flew as a passenger and gave us medical advice. The lack of restrictions was not confined to the medical side. The pilot of today would probably shudder at the thought of flying machines serviced by men who held no ground engineers' licences, and which had no certificate of airworthiness. I was glad to find that my pupils' confidence in me had not been diminished by my accident, and it was not long before they were taking instruction again.

Some days after my return I read an account of an accident in which Sub-Lieut. Smyth-Pigott had been involved. Writing to his hospital I learnt that he, too, had crashed on the Plain while on a flight to Upavon and had had a narrow escape from death. For me this was a time of gloom, but it was soon lightened by news of a happier nature that reached me from California, where a former pupil, Mr. W.M.F. Pendlebury, had joined the American Flying Corps as an instructor. After consoling me on my accident, he told me that he found the pay good – £25 a month with food and board found – and the Curtiss machines easy to fly.

Perhaps my most interesting pupil of 1914 was tall and lanky J.B. Lucas, son of a former mayor of Kingston-on-Thames, whose legs were so long that he could not operate the rudder properly from the seat. His knees were almost under his chin. I found it more convenient for him to sit in the passenger seat, stretch his legs astride of me and grip the joystick over my shoulders. He was so optimistic that I found him very difficult to teach. Unhappily for my lanky friend the war intervened before he could complete his tuition, and his flying ambitions were never realized. The next I heard of him was that he had joined Kitchener's Army.

On April 8th Sergt. E.N. Deane, a promising beginner, was killed while undergoing tests for his brevet. He had already done his two sets of five figures of eight, descending safely after each set, and had then only to complete a volplane, i.e. glide, from 400 feet. Noticing that the wind was strengthening, I had told him not to go higher than 400 feet, and I was therefore astonished and not a little alarmed to see him continue to climb until he was over 1,000 feet. "He's going to try a spiral", I called out apprehensively to the official observer ... I was right. He began to spiral down to earth, but the nose of his machine dipped steeply and Deane fell out of the plane from over 400 feet to the ground. It was a pathetic piece of over-confidence. He was determined to finish his test with special brilliancy and had made his spiral too steep. He must have been thrown forward against the control column and then been catapulted out. After this accident the Royal Aero Club strongly recommended the fitting of quick-release safety-belts, but most pilots still objected to being strapped in.

Although it had killed a man, the accident had taught me something. Though horror-struck while watching I could not help noticing the graceful way the aeroplane had fluttered like a piece of paper to the ground after the pilot had fallen out. It landed, after stalling, tail first and gently concertinaed. The seats were not damaged at all. It struck me that, if the pilot were helpless and yet did not touch the controls while gliding, the machine was not likely to perform any sudden or dangerous manoeuvre. I decided to try out this idea at a slightly higher altitude. When I did I was amazed to find that I could practically hover at the point of stall and could even pancake down to quite a low altitude before dropping the nose and gliding into the aerodrome. I tried it with and without the engine, but I much preferred to switch-off and, with the propeller stopped, float down to the ground with practically no forward speed.

At the end of June, Mr. H.G. Hawker, a pupil of Mr. Sopwith, had a narrow escape while attempting to loop the loop without using his engine so as to see how slowly he could go over the top. Unfortunately, he failed to attain sufficient speed and stalled upside down at just over 1,000 feet. The Sopwith Tabloid he was flying went into an inverted spin, from which Hawker managed to recover only a few feet above the ground, the plane disappearing from view in a steep dive behind some tall trees. Fearing the worst, I rushed over with the others in the school lorry. Luckily, the Tabloid had hit one of the trees, hanging there for a few moments before dropping gently to the ground, and Hawker had stepped out unhurt. Even in his hectic career, this was one of his narrowest shaves.

Among the pupils waiting to pass out from the Bristol School at this time were several who were to become well-known pilots in later days. Midshipman D.S. Don, R.N., was one of them, and it was he who later taught the Prince of Wales, now Duke of Windsor, to fly. I wonder if today he still recalls the gramophone he kept in the rooms he shared with one of the other pupils. To prevent it being used while he was away on leave he always removed the sound-box – little knowing that his room-mate's simple remedy was to "borrow" the sound-box from the Blue Bird's gramophone and keep Don's instrument blaring forth its melodies to his heart's content.

Two other pupils were Lieut. L.F. Richard, who was severely wounded while flying with the R.F.C. in France, but later became Chief Aerodrome Officer at Croydon, and Lieut. B.E. Smythies, who, after a successful war career in which he won the D.F.C., was killed taking off for a flight in 1931. Smythies' accident would have been considered ridiculous if it had not ended so fatally. He ran into a grass roller which was obscured from his vision.

About this time a noticeable slackness became evident in all the schools. As applications for tuition dwindled almost to nothing, I began to hear rumours that the Salisbury School would be closed down and its personnel and equipment transferred to Brooklands. I paid no serious attention to these rumours, but my complacency was rudely awakened one morning at the end of June 1914 when I received a letter from Mr. White, managing director of the Bristol Company, expressing his extreme regret at having to give me one month's notice. In a personal letter sent with the formal notice of dismissal Mr. White said that, though the Company was extremely satisfied with my work, their staff had to be reduced and I, as the junior, had to go. I know that this action must have hurt Mr. White. As was right and proper, my position was later filled by M. Jullerot, who had been with the firm longer than I had.

This was bad luck, but, with aviation firms struggling along and only just keeping their heads above water, I was not alone in my predicament. Feeling that it was no use worrying, I set to work in my remaining month to finish the tuition of my last eighteen pupils. In doing this I was somewhat handicapped by the fact that Stutt, my then assistant, was so short. It was only with great difficulty that he could reach the rudder-bar on the box-kites, and, consequently, I could only entrust him with the very elementary stages of instruction. Among these last eighteen were Second-Lieut. C.E.G. Rabagliati and Lieut. C.W. Wilson, who, with the former as pilot, brought down the first German plane on August 24th 1914. Mr. Harold Treloar also belonged to this group. After gaining his brevet, Treloar left for Australia and later served with the Australian Flying Corps in Mesopotamia, where he was shot down by rifle fire and remained a prisoner of war in Turkey for three years. Only recently I had a message from Treloar delivered to me by J.W. Trevelyan, a pioneer air mechanic and now an "A" licence pilot, who had run across him in Australia. One last name deserves special mention – that of Maurice E.A. Wright. He was an unusually adaptable pupil, and it was much to my regret that he was unable to attend regularly for tuition and that I was unable to complete his course. Considering that he had flown the Ogilvie-Wright glider in 1910, his adaptability was not surprising. He obtained his brevet with the R.N.A.S. at the beginning of the First World War and later became a director of the Fairey Aviation Company.

On July 31st 1914 my engagement with the British and Colonial Aeroplane Company terminated. Leaving M. Jullerot in charge, I made a very sorrowful exit from the old school. On August 4th, as I was returning from an interview with Mr. G. de Havilland and Mr. Holt Thomas at Hendon, I saw on the placards that war had been declared.

Chapter 11

Best in the World

Before relating my own experiences during the First World War it would be as well to review briefly the position regarding pilots in which this country found itself on the outbreak of hostilities.

From January 1st 1913 to August 4th 1914, the total output of trained pupils in Great Britain, including two Service schools, was 143. For the first time the Vickers School, with 36 against the Bristol Company's 35, headed the list of pupils trained during the year, but our output had suffered through the accident which kept me away from duty for six weeks. However, taking the whole period under review, not only had the Bristol Company, headed by Sir George White, taught almost half the total number of pilots trained at British schools, but it had also established an enviable reputation for sound instruction. As Mr. R. Dallas Brett categorically states in his *History of British Aviation, 1908-14*:

> A Bristol pupil felt that he was superior to a pupil trained elsewhere, and he was justified in so feeling. Bristol pupils found it easier to obtain employment in the industry than did those of the other schools, for it was universally recognized that Bristol tuition was the best obtainable anywhere in the world.

During this period, I had given instruction to at least 200 pupils, of whom about 142 were now naval and military officers and from whom more joined the Royal Naval Air Service early in the war. I experienced great satisfaction in watching my one-time "fledglings" soar – many of them to meteoric heights, and I could not help feeling that my work had been of some national importance.

The R.N.A.S. could boast of some excellent pilots in the very early days of the war, but, owing to the great reluctance of senior Admiralty officers to adopt the new air arm, no conspicuous progress was marked overseas for some time. This, however, had its advantages, for there was much to be done at home in the way of patrols and escorts to troop-ships and other shipping across the Channel. The Military Wing of the R.F.C., on the other hand, was treated from the start as an integral part of the army, and almost all its officers and men went with the British Expeditionary Force in August to France and were in battle eight days later.

At the outbreak of the First World War the R.F.C., Military Wing, had only four squadrons ready to go on active service. They were Nos. 2, 3, 4 and 5, with a total officer pilot strength of approximately 90, of whom 29 were my pupils. The names of these 29 were: Majors Higgins, Longcroft, Raleigh; Captains or Lieutenants Waldron, Todd, Rodwell, Spence, Joubert de la Ferte, Read, Christie, Shekleton, Pretyman, MacNeece-Foster, Shephard, Cogan, Playfair, Atkinson, Mills, Mulchay-Morgan, Hosking, Roche, Lewis, Carmichael, Grey, Glanville, Penn-Gaskell, Rabagliati, Boger and Thompson.

I had offered my services to the Royal Naval Air Service, but, mindful of the fact that a previous application for a commission in the R.N.A.S. Reserve, had been turned down because of my eyesight, I accepted an invitation by Jimmy Valentine, a popular pioneer aviator, to visit Major Trenchard, who was then in command at Farnborough. We submitted ourselves for active service, but, on returning to the Royal Aero Club, I found a note instructing me to report to the Air Department of the Admiralty. Feeling very hopeful, I set off at once. On my arrival Lieut. E. Maude informed me that I was to be given a commission, either as Flight-Lieutenant or Flight Commander, and that I should be wanted for instructional duty at Hendon. In the meantime, rather than waste a moment, I assisted with instructional work at the Grahame-White School at Hendon, where Claude Grahame-White had been made a Flight Commander.

The second officer of the R.F.C. to be wounded in the First World War – to the best of my recollection – was one of my early pupils – and a brilliant one – Capt. H.H. Shott. While at Hendon I was delighted to see the announcement that Skene, my late pupil and able assistant, had been given an immediate commission in the R.F.C. with No. 3 Squadron, but my joy was short lived. He was the first officer of the R.F.C. to be killed in France in a crash, and his death was shortly followed by another crash in which an old associate at Brooklands, Lieut. Copland Perry, was killed with his mechanic, Parfitt, in that flying death-trap, the B.E.8.

The days were passing, and, as I had heard nothing further from the Admiralty about my promised appointment, I decided to ask for an interview with the Director of the Naval Air Service. Arrived at the Admiralty, I asked if I might see Capt. Murray Sueter. My request was granted, and Capt. Sueter received me cordially. It was just as well he did, for I needed something to help me overcome the bitter disappointment I met. It was as I half feared; they were unable to accept me on account of my poor eyesight. I contended that my pre-war work had shown that my eyesight had never really affected my flying and that, at such a critical time, it should surely be possible to cut the red tape. It was of no avail. Capt. Sueter was so obviously grieved at having to turn me down that when I left the Admiralty, sick at heart, I felt he might still have something up his sleeve. He had, and three days later I learnt what it was: the Admiralty were prepared to offer me a post as civilian instructor to the Naval Air Service. Though the prospect of having to remain instructing when most of my friends were with squadrons at the front was a bitter pill to swallow, I accepted immediately. Without delaying a moment I reported to Squadron Commander Porte at Hendon and collected my blue badge with the inscription "On War Service, 1914".

Mine was a unique position. I was the only civilian flying instructor appointed to the R.N.A.S., and I received the same pay and allowances as a flight-lieutenant. When I had spare time I went through the usual drills with the sub-lieutenants.

In the meantime Brooklands had been converted into an R.F.C. base. The Blue Bird was now a canteen, and all the familiar figures of those happy pre-war days had left. I heard that Jack Alcock who later made the first direct crossing of the North Atlantic, had been seen presenting a dismal picture as he sat on a petrol can, with his face buried in his hands, mourning the loss of his beloved Farman, which had been commandeered. If only I could have told him that his precious machine had been handed over to me, I am sure he would have been consoled, for we were good friends. When eventually his Farman was broken up I retained the joystick as a souvenir. That joystick is famous for the number of prominent pilots who handled it when pupils. Among them were Warneford, R.M. Groves, J. Bird, J.P. Coleman, E.J. Hodsoll, R. Graham, R.M. Field, E. Cadbury of the Cadbury firm, and Tom England. Alcock also joined the R.N.A.S. and was appointed for instructional duty to Eastchurch, where we both experienced the same difficulty in having to re-instruct pupils who were supposed to have learned to fly before they joined the Service.

Flight-Lieut. E. Bentley Bauman was the first to take charge of the R.N.A.S. station at Hendon, and it was during his short term as C.O. that Flight-Lieut. R.T. Gates was killed. Before obtaining his commission Gates had been Grahame-White's manager, and he was quite new to Service discipline. The full story of how he came to be killed in a night landing has never been told, but I believe that, acting on a sudden impulse, he took a machine up one night early in August 1914 in search of what he believed to be an enemy aircraft. It appeared that he had seen unusual lights "popping about in the heavens", lights which turned out to be signals from Service observation balloons. Had he first reported his suspicions he might have been with us today.

In my new duties I found that I had a variety of aircraft to deal with, most of which had more power than those I had previously flown. They included a 100 h.p. Deperdussin monoplane, a 100 h.p. (Anzani) Handley-Page biplane, a 70 h.p. Caudron biplane and several B.E.s and Maurice Farmans. As I still held the view that box-kites were the best for elementary instruction, we retained one or two of these machines for this purpose. There was also a good deal of variety about my work. Testing the aircraft was my first concern, and next came the testing of those probationary officers from the civilian schools who had recently taken their brevets. Many of these young men had haphazard ways of flying because they had been made to take their tests after too hurried teaching. It was one of my jobs to sort out those who were unsuitable for Service flying and to try to knock the others into shape. The most difficult pupils to teach were those who had been trained on tractors, whereas the best pupils came from the Grahame-White school, where Chief Instructor Marcus Manton, a well-known early aviator, was using box-kites. As instructional machines the box-kites proved their worth over and over again – in the very same manner, I should imagine, as the de Havilland Tiger Moth trainers did in the Second World War. In fact, the so-called advanced pupils trained on tractors gave more trouble than those beginners who were sent in shoals from the Admiralty Air Department to learn from the very beginning.

There are few theatre-goers, I dare guess, who realize that Ben Travers was a naval pilot during the First World War. He came to me as a probationary sub to learn to fly and was, I regret to say, one of my most difficult pupils. He was big-hearted and fearless but had not, to start with, the slightest gift of "feel". We had a number of exciting experiences together. One occurred when I was making a test flight with him before handing over for a solo. We had reached a height of about 80 feet when I suddenly felt cables dangling round my legs and the control column. Looking over the side, I was amazed to see the ailerons flapping about in the most alarming manner. If we had started to turn, this mishap might well have spelt disaster. Luckily we were still in straight flight with plenty of room ahead to land. Needless to say, I lost no time in switching-off and putting the nose down to land, in the meantime keeping the plane level by vigorous "pedipulation" of the rudder. The gentle smoothness of our landing was in striking contrast to the fury of my feelings as I strode off to the sheds to find out who was responsible for not ensuring the cables were in airworthy condition before the test.

Ben Travers later assisted me with elementary instruction and eventually became a steady and reliable pilot. He was most popular as an officer, and his entertaining abilities were always in demand.

Chapter 12

Piling up the Hours

In the earlier days of the First World War there was a sprinkling of senior naval staff officers at the Admiralty who wanted their wings. One of them was Commander R.M. Groves, then O.C. Naval Air Stations. He soon became known as "The Crasher". After he had finished his elementary tuition I found it difficult to keep any control over him. When I was not on duty or engaged with other pupils, he used his discretion – or, should I say, indiscretion – to take up any machine he fancied, usually with lamentable results. He caused me a great deal of anxiety, and I was most relieved when he gained his brevet. It was well known that he smashed more aircraft during his training than any other naval pupil at Hendon at this time, and it was surprising that he was not killed or even injured. At the same time he was greatly admired for his human qualities and because he was by no means a young man. Commander Groves was a sportsman all the way, and, as I found in the case of Warneford, who gained the V.C. for destroying a Zeppelin, he had a keen eye for a good pilot. Had it not been for Groves, I am certain that Warneford would never have had the chance to display his valour.

Warneford was then a probationary officer pupil at Hendon. Squadron Commander Sitwell, a pukka navy man who was drilled in its strict school of discipline, took the view that Warneford would never make an officer from the disciplinarian point of view, and he was about to send a report to headquarters to that effect. I had insisted that I was more than satisfied with his flying. Warneford was, in fact, a born aviator. He had mastered the intricacies of flight with amazing swiftness, and, as he was completely without fear, my only difficulty was to check his over-confidence. I knew that only a special effort would get Warneford through, so, during a chance visit by Commander Groves, I seized the opportunity to ask Warneford to make the best show he could before him. The Commander was so impressed by Warneford's brilliant flying that he made the remark: "This youngster will either do big things or kill himself." It is sad indeed that, when the time came, he could not do the one without the other.

Sitwell and I often disagreed over these beginners. I thought he carried his discipline too far, and his strictness seemed to me to frighten some of the boys so much that it hindered their flying progress. In my opinion they needed happy, unhampered minds and good spirits to be able to concentrate on their lessons. My job was to select and produce first-class pilots, and to this aim I strove – regardless of other considerations.

Early in January 1915 the first rumours reached us of an approaching aerial invasion of London, and, as the Germans had recently been active in the neighbourhood of the Belgian coast, this did not seem at all unlikely. It is a striking commentary on the confusion of thought that existed in those days about aerial defence that, while the Government let it be known they considered our defensive preparations so strong and elaborate that the enemy would find any such attempt too costly, they nevertheless gave orders for us and all the other training establishments, who were no part of their preparations and could be of little value, to stand by for action. Our machines were none of them equipped with offensive weapons of any kind, but everyone who could fly, including me, the only civilian, got ready to take off, each accompanied by a passenger armed with a rifle. The rifles even included those used by the sub-lieutenants for drilling. Luckily, this aerial invasion proved to be only another of the many abortive rumours of those days, but, when I think of the way aerial warfare has since developed, I cannot resist a smile at the idea of our makeshift squadron with its makeshift rifles roaring into the air against the might of Germany.

Sir Winston Churchill was an early flying enthusiast and, some-time before the outbreak of the war, had taken lessons from Spencer Grey, a pioneer naval aviator. While First Lord of the Admiralty he made a tour of inspection of our aerodrome, staff and pupils, and it was while he was leaving the cockpit of my machine and stepped on my hand that I first learnt that he carried a lot of weight in more ways than one.

Whatever the First Lord thought, I found myself pleased with the work being done at Hendon, and I heard from good authority at the Air Department that they were not unsatisfied either. With shoals of pupils arriving weekly, I was becoming busier every day. My hours in the air were ticking away like the stages on a taximeter, and the morning group of pupils eagerly waiting for their turn of tuition was reminiscent of children round an ice-cream barrow. There was no keeping them away.

I recall here an ace pupil, Flight Commander T.N. Gerrard (Figure 32). A sub when I taught him to fly, he made good operational use of his skill and soon earned promotion. During one of his air combats while he was flying a triplane he became engaged in a close, lone tussle with a whole squadron of German aircraft. In spite of the odds he brought down two of them, but by this time enemy fire had practically destroyed the whole of his top plane, leaving him, in effect, with a biplane. However, he got back safely to enjoy many another combat and was later awarded the D.S.C. for this feat. After this demonstration of the battle value of having three planes on one machine one is inclined to wonder why triplanes were so soon abandoned later for aerial warfare.

Chapter 13

Chingfliers

Early in 1915 we moved to new quarters at Chingford (Figure 33), about ten miles from London, where I was given the job of ferrying the aircraft. They were of many different types, the most interesting being an old Handley Page which in the air resembled a German Taube. Before I set course for Chingford in this Handley Page I had decided to climb fairly high in case we should be mistaken for an enemy aircraft; but my engine was not pulling too well, so, after wasting twenty minutes flying over the aerodrome in a vain effort to gain height, I made up my mind to chance it. As we were nearing Chingford at quite a low altitude my pupil attracted my attention to puffs of smoke in the distance which were coming towards us. I could see that the firing came from a Small-Arms factory near my destination, and taking evasive action, we flew low round the aerodrome and sideslipped in from the opposite side. Since many of the officers there were unable to identify us, we found on landing that our appearance had caused something of a stir in the station. That is what often used to happen in the days before aircraft recognition schools and radiolocation – and what still happens occasionally in spite of them.

Chingford was a pleasant change from the crowded conditions of Hendon. School work could now be carried out without interference from other aircraft. The one drawback, and I am not so sure it really was a drawback, was the smallness of the airfield. It was even smaller than Brooklands and was surrounded by a reservoir, streams and swamps. Though it had its advantages, in that pupils were forced to learn how to land in a restricted area, I was nevertheless surprised that it had been chosen as an airfield. At Hendon there had been other civilians to keep me company. At Chingford I was the only one, and I felt rather a fish out of water. When I joined the officers in the Mess I certainly felt very much out of things in my civilian clothes, but I was in the Service in practically every other way, even to saluting the colours at daybreak and sunset.

Our first Commanding Officer at Chingford was a charming man and beloved by all. He was Flight-Lieut. C. Pulford and had been lent to the R.N.A.S. by the Royal Navy. On applying for a flying course in 1912 he had been ticked off by his captain for entertaining "such a crazy idea, which had no future and would lead to no advancement". He persisted, however, and obtained his brevet at the Central Flying School in January 1915. In spite of the fact that I was with Pulford at Chingford for only a few weeks, I often remember him, with the rest of us, flying by day and standing-by all night to chase Zeppelins. But, strenuous though this life was, it had its amusing moments. I remember one day, while Pulford was standing by my machine and I was running up the engine, a cylinder flew off and whizzed through the air into the side of a wooden hut belonging to a naval officer. I thought Pulford would never stop laughing at the sight of the startled and stark naked figure which came rushing out of the door. Judging by his language, this hardy mariner did not approve of being disturbed in this way while he was in his bath.

At this time I was flying from early morning until late in the evening, resting only when the weather was unfit for flying. Except for elementary instruction on the box-kites, it was no longer necessary to watch the weather quite so closely as it had been in the Brooklands days. With their greater power and stability, the Avros, Blériots, Bristol Bullets, Shorts and other of our aircraft were able to fly in most conditions, and so I rarely got out of one machine except to clamber into another or stretch my limbs for a minute or two. Instruments, then, were just beginning to come into use. They often failed completely, and, although we had to teach pupils their use, it was still very necessary to ensure they could fly without them.

Incidentally, the old Handley Page I mentioned at the beginning of this chapter was so stable that it was of little value for teaching pupils the sense of "feel", and it was apt to make pilots a little over-confident. It was eventually crashed at Chingford by a pilot who relied too much on its inherent stability. Moreover, to train a pupil on a very stable aeroplane to be a war pilot would be like expecting a man to win the Grand National after only riding a cart horse. In those days of acute shortage of aircraft for any purpose, we had, of course, to take any machines we could get, and the history of this Handley Page furnishes an example of the sort of thing that used to happen. Acquired, with its early type 100 h.p. Anzani engine, in the opening months of 1913 by Mr. Rowland Ding, it took part with him in most of the aviation meetings that year and also carried Princess Lowenstein Wertheim across the Channel. In 1914 it was bought by the R.N.A.S. and so came into my hands, but, before coming to this it had flown 10,000 miles and carried over 200 passengers. Officially, it was to be used for both training and defence, but for the latter purpose its armament consisted of only one Webley revolver – worn by the pilot. Nevertheless, during the early months of the war I found it quite valuable for observation patrols by day and not entirely without use for advanced instruction. After the crash in 1915 it was written off, but I still retain its propeller boss as a frame for the altimeter, one of the first ever made, given me by Lord Edward Grosvenor.

After I had been at Chingford about a fortnight I received orders to report to the Admiralty. No reason was given, and on my way there I thought I might perhaps be "on the mat" because of my views on naval discipline. I was therefore doubly pleased when Capt. Sueter gave me the good news that I was to be commissioned as a Flight-Lieut. and that an eyesight test would be waived. Needless to say, there was a grand celebration in our Mess that night, and the champagne flowed freely. Congratulations appeared in *Flight,* and I learned there that Lewis Turner and C. Howard Pixton had also been granted commissions in the R.F.C.

About this time we were all tremendously thrilled to hear of Sub-Lieut. Warneford's encounter with the Zeppelin which he chased, bombed and destroyed single-handed near Ghent. After the action he had been forced to land through a petrol leak in enemy territory and, after pouring the remaining fuel from his riddled tank into his sound one, had flown back safely through a hail of fire. It was for this action he was awarded his V.C. Coming so soon after this brilliant exploit, his death a few days later was all the more tragic. With an American journalist as passenger, he was making a right-hand turn at about 700 feet when his aeroplane was struck by a sudden gust and sideslipped. Neither Warneford nor his passenger were strapped in, and both were thrown out. His passenger was killed immediately, and Warneford died on the way to hospital.

His body was brought to England for burial at Brompton Cemetery, where full naval honours were accorded by the R.N.A.S. The Director of Naval Air Service, Capt. Murray Sueter, was present. Together with a party of pupils I also attended, and I shall never forget the vast crowds that assembled there to pay him their last respects.

Happily, all our accidents were not so tragic: some, indeed, were not without a touch of humour. It was well that this was so, for, without a touch of humour here and there, however light, it would have been impossible to carry on. It happened one day, when I was preparing to take off with a pupil, no mechanic was available to start the engine. I was sitting in the passenger seat, and the pupil, having, as I thought, set the throttle and switches, got out to swing the propeller. As the engine started up with a roar I saw that the throttle was too far open. Being rather short in the arms, I was unable to reach it from my seat, and by the time I had managed to scramble over into the pilot's seat the machine was travelling forward at a good pace towards some of the other aircraft. My pupil, in the meantime, had been rolled over by the tail boom and was sitting in the dust, bedraggled and not a little startled. I reached the rudder-bar just in time to swerve past another aeroplane. It was no use trying to stop, for I was nearly at the edge of the river, so I opened the throttle wide and, as we came to the river, I heaved. Luck was with me, my machine staggered off into the air in the nick of time, and I was able to do a circuit and collect my pupil again.

It was only a few days later that Ince, a young Canadian, stopped his prop while coming in to land in a J.N.4. Curtiss. Not wishing to call out a mechanic, as he was some distance from the sheds, he got out and swung the propeller himself – forgetting to close the throttle. For the first time, I imagine, in the history of the Curtiss engine, this one started straight away and revved up. After knocking Ince over, the machine then proceeded to take off on its own. Flying down the centre of the aerodrome about ten feet up, it made a gentle right-hand turn with exactly the correct amount of bank and flew over the brook. Then, as if prompted by some devilish whim, it suddenly turned straight for the armament store. The armament store was full of bombs and fuses, and the plane caught it fair and square in the middle. There were about 100 people on the aerodrome, and, when the plane hit the store, they flattened themselves on the ground with their hands over their ears like a pack of cards. But the machine was the only thing that exploded!

As I have mentioned previously in this book, good air-mechanics were comparatively few, although all were as keen as mustard. They did the best they could with their limited experience, but it was not wise to rely on them too much, nor was it fair to them to do so. I used to lecture them on the need for thoroughness in their work and remind them that we were to a great extent at their mercy when in the air. I often took the mechanics up on flights when testing aircraft and found them quick to appreciate the pilot's point of view. From the ground personnel generally I never refused a request for a flight if I could possibly help it, and hundreds of them must have flown with me from time to time. These little trips helped them all – doctors, padres, ground officers and mechanics – to appreciate the difference between the attitude of the men who fly and those on the ground. A difference of attitude there definitely is, and, unless this is understood, many a good pilot can be lost to the flying Services through his inability to conform with the dictates of a more stereotyped ground officer.

Among the senior pupils of my Chingford days there were two I remember almost as well as "Crasher" Groves. They were Commander C.L. Lambe and Capt. W.L. Elder, both R.N. Lambe was another "not so young" pupil, but one whose cool head and steady nerve overcame the handicap of having to learn somewhat later in life. In due course he became a very sound pilot and later he rose to high rank.

"Daddy" Elder, as we called him – though not, of course, to his face – was very slow but persevering. He was most anxious not to let his seniority and special requirements interfere with the school routine. He left it to me to fit in his tuition at the most convenient times and would ring up frequently to see when he should come along. We eventually arranged for him to come in the evenings about half an hour before sunset. He lived near Hendon, and when he was nearly ready for his brevet tests we used to fly him back to the Hendon aerodrome. One evening, having left it rather late before starting, we ran into a thick mist half way. Though darkness was fast approaching, I decided to make the best of it and press on. To find our way we had to fly so low that I could almost see into the signal boxes on the railway and even had to dodge the higher trees and roof-tops. Things became so bad that, when I spotted a suitable field, I decided to lob down and not attempt to find the aerodrome. I made the landing safely, but, hearing from some people who approached us that Hendon aerodrome was "only a few fields away", I foolishly decided to make a hop over to it. Immediately we were again airborne I realized that "a few fields away" was no more reliable than most people's "just round the corner". There was, of course, no sign of the aerodrome, and it was darker than ever. I did, however, spot the Edgware Road, and, hugging it as low as I dared, I followed it to the familiar Handley Page works. After that it was just a case of looking for the aircraft factory at the corner of Collingdale Avenue, on the left. Having picked this up, we flew straight into the aerodrome close over the tops of the hangars and landed safely. As we were long overdue, everyone was much relieved. "Daddy" Elder was so pleased with his adventurous trip and its happy ending that he promptly invited me home to supper. He took his brevet in August 1915, and was later sent to command an important station in France.

It may have seemed rather absurd for these senior officers to take up flying – indeed, many people said so at the time – but I admired their pluck and courage and considered it all important that those who had to take active command of air units should have practical experience of the problems of their pilots and air crews. At the same time I must confess that we found it a bit of a strain instructing and flying them about while distracted by the thought of what might happen to us if we happened to "prang" a brass hat.

This episode with "Daddy" Elder was not the last of my experiences of flying with senior officers in awkward situations. It was, indeed, with another senior officer – and this time a "double brass" – that I was again trapped by mist in the Thames valley, and on this occasion we were not made any happier by the knowledge that we were right over some anti-aircraft batteries. The Ack-Ack men could not see clearly enough to identify us, and, fearing we might be hostile, they rang up the Admiralty. The Admiralty then rang Chingford to ask if any of their planes were up. The C.O., knowing that I was the only one flying and never thinking I would then be over the Thames valley, recommended that the guns should fire. They did, but we arrived back at the station unscratched.

Chapter 14

First Zeppelin Raid

On the night of May 15th 1915, there took place the first Zeppelin raid on London. As usual, the unpreparedness of our forces to deal with these enemy raids was the subject of a public outcry. The best Service aeroplane we had at that time was the B.E.2c, a general favourite with the pilots because it was easy to fly and able to remain in the air for a considerable time, but lacking speed and climb. Unless luck was very much on their side, pilots in B.E.2c's were no match for the Zeppelins at night. But we were even more handicapped on the ground. Our night landing facilities, such as they were, could hardly have been more dangerous, and it was to their inadequacy that we owed most of our casualties in night operations. For these deficiencies in the air and on the ground there were excuses that could be accepted by those aware of our circumstances, but there was another weakness for which there was no reasonable excuse, and that was the hesitancy of the Government in deciding who should have charge of London's air defences. It was a good thing Germany did not possess as many Zeppelins as we supposed or she would have been able to inflict far more damage while the pundits at Whitehall continued to argue. I took a personal part in the first night raid over London, as well as in most of the others that followed, and can truly say they were dangerous and nerve-wracking ordeals.

On this memorable first night, orders had already come through for all available pilots and aircraft to stand by, and, with them we received instructions that, should we encounter a Zeppelin and fail to destroy it with our rifles and hand grenades, we were to ram it!

25. Gustav Hamel's last appearance at Brooklands before the First World War in his Blériot monoplane.

26. M. Jullerot, Manager and Chief Instructor at the Bristol School, Larkhill, Salisbury, about to test a new type of tractor biplane with the Author (in flying helmet) as passenger, 1913.

27. Crawford-Kehrmann's crash at Brooklands in a Bristol biplane: (*left to right*) Lt. A.E. Morgan, Graham Harris, Lt. Crawford-Kehrmann and Lt. M.W. Duncan.

28. The Author about to take off in a Bristol monoplane on the flight which finished in the sewage farm at Brooklands, 1912.

29. The wrecked Bristol monoplane in which G.L. Gipps was killed at Larkhill in 1914.

30. The first Army aeroplane to land in France during the First World War. The B.E.2a and pilot, Major H. Harvey-Kelly, D.S.O., at Lythe, Yorkshire.

31. Three Australians with Geoffrey England and Collyns Pizey at Larkhill, Salisbury, 1911. Captain Penfold is in the pilot's seat with Eric Harrison and Harry Busteed on the left.

32. Sub-Lieutenant T.N. Gerrard in a Maurice Farman biplane at Hendon, 1915.

33. The Royal Naval Air Service Station at Chingford, 1915. The aircraft include a Grahame-White Box-kite, a Maurice Farman Shorthorn, an Avro 504K, a B.E.2c and a Curtiss JN.

34. Commander R.B. Ward R.N. and the Author in the first dual-control Grahame-White Box-kite at Chingford, 1915.

35. Norman Blackburn's crash on the edge of the reservoir near Chingford, 1915.

36. The Grahame-White biplane in which Flight Officer Louis Lavigne was killed at Chingford, 1917.

37. The Sopwith Baby seaplane being lowered from the jetty, R.N.A.S. Cattewater, 1917.

38. A Sopwith Baby in flight.

39. A Short 225 seaplane on patrol, 1915.

40. A Sopwith 1½-Strutter taking off from a platform fitted to the guns of a British warship, 1917.

41. An SSZ non-rigid airship of the Royal Naval Air Service escorting a convoy, 1918.

42. The Avro seaplane (110 h.p. le Rhône engine) at Ventnor, Isle of Wight, 1919.

43. Being towed to the moorings off Ventnor Pier with Sir A. Verdon Roe standing on the wing.

44. The Saunders Kittiwake on a trial flight in 1921. It was the first all-wood amphibian to be constructed but never went into production.

45-46. The Merriam-Newman glider built for the *Daily Mail* gliding competition at Itford Hill, Sussex, 1922. The machine crashed shortly after taking off.

47. The Author flying the Lowe-Wylde glider at East Cowes, Isle of Wight, 1923.

48. Adjusting the rudder of the Merriam-Newman glider before the *Daily Mail* glider competition in 1922.

49. Experimenting with launching a glider by a tow rope stretched between two motorcars, at East Cowes, 1930.

50. The Author with the famous Gnome 50 h.p. engine, 1912.

The fact that most of the Chingford pilots had very little flying experience by day and practically none by night worried me considerably. With this in mind, although, after a long day at tuition and testing I was supposed to be off duty, I decided to join the others. There was a toss up as to who should fly with me. Sub-Lieut. J.S. Morrison won and was my observer on the 100 h.p. Deperdussin monoplane. This particular aeroplane was a brute to land in a small aerodrome by day, let alone by night, and was dangerous even in capable hands. As a forced landing would more than likely entail a serious crash, night flying was far from appealing. In addition to the gun and grenades carried by Morrison I had a revolver which was lent to me by Sub-Lieut. Thompson.

When the alarm finally came through we took off in a thick ground mist and flew over Central London. There we cruised about for two hours without seeing a sign of a "gas-bag" anywhere. At the end of these two hours the light on my dashboard failed, and I was unable to read any of my instruments. In spite of what I have written earlier about instruments I must admit that they are a great help to flying by night. Seeing the faint outline of the Thames below and taking a rough bearing from the stars, I headed back in the general direction of the aerodrome. Goodness knows how I ever reached it. What lights I could see were very dim and scattered, and, when eventually I found myself near Chingford, I had been flying for a long period and, with no means of checking the fuel gauge, was beginning to worry about petrol. At this stage, too, my goggles oiled up, and, as I reached up to wipe them, they flew off. Then, as I came down lower, expecting to see the landing lights, there were none to be seen. After some anxious moments peering through the mist I eventually spotted a sort of flare, and, by doing a steep turn round it, managed to get a vague idea of where we were. There was a blackish pool to one side which I thought might be our reservoir, so, with my eyes bunged up with oil, I cut off the engine and made for the flare. My flying now was entirely by feel. At what I estimated to be five feet above the ground I flattened out and started to pancake so as to reduce my forward speed to a minimum. We landed like a duck on a pond, slightly bending the axle, but otherwise quite safely. It was only when I had got out of the machine that I realized how badly my eyes were affected by the oil, and it was not until they had been treated several times by the M.O. that they recovered.

Thus ended our fruitless errand. We might just as well have stayed at home. The other pilots and observers were not so fortunate. None of the others got back to the aerodrome that night. Douglas M. Barnes was killed, several others crashed, and a number were injured. Ben Travers, observer to Barnes, miraculously escaped with only slight injuries. While we were running these risks in an obviously almost impossible attempt to get to close quarters with the enemy, the raiders were flying far above us and showering their bombs at random over the darkened metropolitan area.

Later on the R.F.C. took over the air defence of London and placed it under command of General R.E.B. Ashmore, one of my early pupils. Just before that happened I had been piloting Commander Brock while he experimented with his then well-known Brock tracer bullets. I offered to patrol in a B.E.2c armed with his new weapon and lie in wait for a Zepp. Much to my disappointment my offer was refused, and the next thing I heard was that Capt. Leefe Robinson, R.F.C., had used these bullets when he brought down a Zepp. in flames at Cuffley.

Among those who met their end in those days while night flying against Zeppelins there was one whose death I regarded as particularly tragic because it was, in a sense, doubly unnecessary. Major Penn-Gaskell, one of my 1912 pupils, was commanding a London Air Defence station when he received orders to send a plane up to meet an expected raid. At this station there were one or two other pilots besides the C.O. with night flying experience available, but, as the night was foggy and dangerous, Penn-Gaskell decided to undertake the duty himself. After the usual two hours or so fruitless search he came down and was killed while attempting to land. It took many accidents like these to convince the authorities that night operations with the equipment and facilities then at our disposal was simply a waste of valuable and gallant lives. The pressure of public opinion was undoubtedly very great, but it is the duty of those in highly responsible positions to resist public opinion when they know it to be ignorant and ill-advised.

At that time there was a great deal of jealousy between the two Air Services. The Navy, probably because it was the Senior Service and also enjoyed more prestige, undoubtedly had the pick of the available aircraft. Although I held a commission in the R.N.A.S. I had an equal interest in the R.F.C., and the majority of my pre-war pupils were in that Service. From time to time I received many reports of the courage and daring of my old friends in action with the R.F.C., and I like to record the following warm tribute paid to these early pilots by Philip Gibbs while war correspondent to the *Daily Telegraph* at General Headquarters of the British Expeditionary Force in 1915:

> This at least can be fairly said. Unless we had had a number of efficient air pilots at the outbreak of the war who were able to raise and train a large body of young enthusiasts with extraordinary rapidity during the war, the work of our armies in the field would have been like blind men fumbling in the dark compared with the present accuracy of their long-range finding. Of the courage of these men of the Royal Flying Corps it is impossible to write too much praise. Scores of times I have seen them with shrapnel bursting all round their planes so that they seemed to be sailing to certain death. They escaped by their own skill or by just the fluke of luck time after time.

One of the best photographs I still retain of this period is of Flight-Lieut. Norman W.C. Blackburn's crash at Chingford (Figure 35). This Blackburn, brother of the pioneer Blackburn, stalled at a good 1,000 feet, nose-dived and crashed into the bank of the reservoir with his tail in the air. His engine was buried 5 feet in the ground. Everyone ran out expecting to find a crumpled body in the wreckage, but, though the seats were concertinaed, there was no sign of a body. We thought he must have been catapulted into the reservoir and just as some of us were preparing to dive into the water a shout came from the road on the other side of the aerodrome. It was from Blackburn. Dripping with water and slime, he was calmly walking back after his "ducking".

That Chingford reservoir, like the sewage farm at Brooklands, could have told many a strange story. So often, in fact, did our pilots and their machines make its acquaintance, that we found it wise to keep a boat permanently moored there in readiness.

The first serious accident to occur at Chingford cast a gloom over the whole station and gave me the most horrible experience of my life. A young probationary officer was flying solo on an Avro when his engine failed. As he could not make the aerodrome he crashed on a rough piece of waste land. His machine caught fire immediately. I had just landed. Seeing the fire and yelling to the men at the sheds to follow, I opened up my engine again, took off and hopped over the river to the scene of the crash. Cecil Murray led the band of men on foot, swimming across the river on the way. But we were all too late. When I jumped out of my machine I found the heat of the blazing plane terrific. We ladled water from the river in helmets, flying caps and coats, but we could not get at the pilot until we were able to wrench the wing off and let him fall through. When Murray and I pulled him clear he was still alive but quite unrecognizable. As we swamped him with oil from the tank of my machine to try to ease his agony, he pleaded with the medical officer to put him out of his misery. He lived for an hour and was conscious to the end. The horror of those first few minutes was so great that it was some time before Murray and I realized that we had both received painful burns pulling the unfortunate pilot clear. This accident had a deep effect on the young pilot officers, and, although few wished to carry on flying that day, I set to work to take as many as possible on short trips in a fast machine. I stunted between thirty and forty of them – a few minutes each – for the rest of the day, and I believe it did much to restore their confidence.

During the time I was at Chingford I lived with my wife in a house nearby which adjoined a large cemetery. At the conclusion of my morning and evening work I would circle round the house to indicate that I would be home in a few minutes. I was therefore much puzzled when I read an entry in one of my pupil's log-books: "Circled two or three times over a cemetery, where Flight-Lieut. Merriam made signs." I suppose he had mistaken my signals to mean something very different! It was the same pupil who one day unaccountably jerked the control column hard forward just after we had flattened out for a landing. Before I could get it back again the nose had hit the ground and I was shot straight out over the elevator (it was a box-kite with the elevator in front) like a shuttlecock. How I failed to break my neck, still remains a mystery. My pupil snapped his safety-belt, but his fall was broken by the struts.

According to an article published in the American magazine *Liberty* some years later, it would appear that I had somehow earned the reputation of being a "make 'em or break 'em" type. Though I do not think this description is quite fair to myself or my methods, the article is amusing enough to reproduce. It was written by A. Roy Brown and entitled "Luck on the Wings":

In the *Red Knight of Germany* recently published an American told of being pitched out of a plane in a dive but of landing back on it, fortunately for him, before reaching the ground. I remember a case that matches it. This happened at Chingford, a training drome in England. A man named Merriam was an instructor there. His method with cadets was to make 'em or break 'em quick. Not that he was hard boiled. No, he was merely an efficiency expert. "Got a sensitive backbone" he'd say to a quirk student as he pulled on his gloves. "Hope so, sir – why sir?" "If you haven't you can't fly. Get in". He never wore goggles. He was very short-sighted and claimed he couldn't see anyway. But he could fly. On this particular occasion his pupil was Tubby Wallace. They went up in a Grahame-White two-seater (this was early in the game), an animated box-kite that looked like a birdcage on wings. It was a pusher type, with a little nacelle instead of a fuselage, in which the instructor sat in front with the quirk behind. They went up to 4,000 or 5,000 feet. Tubby had forgotten to fasten his belt. He did not seem particularly interested. Old Merriam was a crank. He did not know that Tubby's belt was loose, but he did know that he was not very impressed with the lesson. Without warning, to jolt him, Merriam whipped up and over in a sharp loop, and, suddenly, as they flung over coming down, Tubby felt himself leaving the cockpit and starting a vertical dive on his own. He was pitching over the bow earthward. That was nasty. He became interested right away. He got busy trying to clutch something. As he shot over Merriam he managed to wrap his legs around the instructor's neck. He gripped and hung on with his feet locked, nearly choking him. But it would have taken more than that to have fussed old Merriam, who could fly without looking. He pulled out of the loop, glided down and made a perfect landing with Tubby's legs still around his neck and Tubby's head hanging over the front of the nacelle. It was fortunate for Tubby that the machine was a pusher and not a tractor with the propeller in front or he would have been guillotined. It was lucky that he had strong legs or he would have broken his neck. It was lucky that the pilot was Merriam or the pair of them would have crashed. But it taught Tubby to fasten his belt.

I wish I could write exciting stuff like that, without too strict a regard for the facts. Of course no one, even in a nightmare, has ever attempted to loop a box-kite. All I did was to execute a steeply banked turn.

Among my other pupils at this time were Flight Sub-Lieut. L.E. Goble – first, with MacIntyre as observer to fly round Australia, Flight Sub-Lieut. Rae, later chief test pilot to Boulton, Paul Ltd., and the well-known Lieut. Commander P.F.M. Fellowes who later became Aide de Camp to King George V and leader of the Houston Everest Expedition. One Flight Sub-Lieut., H.G. Brackley, eventually became Air Superintendent of Imperial Airways, and another, J.F. Horsey, achieved an enviable reputation as one of Imperial Airways' most outstanding pilots, with a record of hours, I believe, unequalled by any other pilot.

Chapter 15

Quality Before Quantity

When Capt. Murray Sueter, the Creator and Director of Naval Air Services, asked me to speed up I told him I could only do so if I had one or two extra assistants and that to my mind, it was essential that quality should come before quantity. I predicted that it would not be long before we saw the bad results of the failure to observe this principle which I saw going on in other training establishments. He agreed with my views and promised to let me have the extra help I wanted, and I have never ceased to be grateful to him for his far-sightedness. My prediction came painfully true. The R.F.C. and those R.N.A.S. training stations which tried to follow their lead soon began to reap the harvest of their injudicious haste. In the R.F.C. insufficient instruction, particularly in landings, was resulting in the deaths of many young pilots before they had even reached the front, and of others who reached France but crashed before they had gone into action. In the R.N.A.S., so I was told by one of my pupils, a number of Flight Sub-Lieuts. from one of our stations had been posted to a certain front, but on arrival were found to be so untrained that they had to be instructed all over again. Thus, the country was losing some of the cream of its manhood to no purpose, and the active squadrons were only being hindered in their primary role by this attempt to speed up at all costs. Perhaps blame for this state of affairs should not be attributed entirely to the heads of the two Services or their subordinates, but, whoever was ultimately responsible, the whole thing, to my mind, was a scandal.

Though it was still difficult to find pilots with the essential gifts for teaching, I had an admirable little band of assistants, all of whom had originally been my pupils. There were seven of them, all Flight-Lieuts. – Ben Travers, J.S. Mills, C.H. Hayward, G.H. Jackson, J.C. Mitchell, Cecil Murray and L. Morgan. As evidence of the value of our thorough methods I think I may be forgiven for saying that, compared with other training establishments, we had very few fatal accidents and that we turned out an unusual number of distinguished war pilots. One of the most distinguished of our Chingford vintages was Roy Brown, the Flight Commander who is now acknowledged to have brought down the "Red Knight", Baron von Richthofen [now thought to have been a bullet fired from the ground]. He was a Canadian and, I am proud to say, one of my own pupils. Another Chingford pupil, Flight-Lieut. M.A. Harker, was flying with Brown that day. Richthofen's famous circus, numbering on this occasion twenty-three Fokker triplanes, was encountered at 10,000 feet about six miles behind the German lines by a British formation of fifteen Sopwith Camels and two S.E.5s. May, a new-comer to the squadron, soon found himself well below the others – a fatal mistake often made by new pilots, and Richthofen, seeing his opportunity, made a bee-line for him. But Brown, noticing his protege in difficulties, went after them and, with a single burst, shot the "Red Knight" through the heart and head. For this gallant and decisive action Brown was awarded a bar to his D.S.C. and it was pinned on him by the Prince of Wales himself.

Two of our other pupils, Flight-Lieuts. Leckie and Galpin, were credited with being the first to destroy a Zeppelin by machine-gun fire from a flying-boat – the L 22. They had shown the greatest promise while training, and both rose to important positions later.

Lieut.-Col. Robertson, another distinguished pilot who had been through our hands, enjoyed one war-time experience of an unusually pleasant nature. While piloting a flying-boat in the Channel he was shot down after an encounter with five German sea-planes. The pilot of one of the German machines landed alongside the wreckage, told Robertson he was near the English coast and asked him whether he wished to return as prisoner of war or would rather wait on the off chance that some British aircraft would pick him up. On hearing that he wished to stay with the wreckage, the German pilot took a photograph of him, waved a cheery farewell and flew back towards Zeebrugge. Colonel Robertson was picked up and is now, incidentally, in charge of Prestwick airport.

Earlier in this chapter I mentioned that Chingford, during my time, was remarkably free from serious accidents. While this was true, comparatively speaking, we did experience some unfortunate incidents. Two machines, for instance, collided in the air, but both pilots, having kept their heads, managed to land their damaged aircraft safely. We were not always so lucky. Not long after, Flight-Lieut. Lewis Morgan, with his pupil, Flight Officer Randolph Seed, was killed while giving instruction on a Maurice Farman "Longhorn". The machine suddenly dived into the ground, obviously out of control. I think it was due to the propeller breaking and smashing the tail boom and then jamming the controls. I say this because the same thing had happened to me before the war, but I was fortunate in that the jammed controls kept the aircraft at a gliding angle, thus enabling us to land, though heavily. On this day it was mere chance that I was not killed instead of Morgan, for I had been teaching on this machine all the morning and had handed it over only a few minutes before the accident occurred. Morgan was a most efficient instructor, and his death was a severe blow to us all.

At this time we had a few American volunteers who termed themselves Canadians, and, of course, we were also getting a large number of true Canadians. They were a fine lot of chaps and took to flying with such gusto that it was a job to hold them back. Leckie, Roy Brown, J.A. Glen, R.F. Redpath, K.F. Saunders, are just a few of the names of these men from overseas to whom we owe so much. Typical of the letters I received from them – and still do – was one from Redpath asking me: "Do you still eat apples in the early morning?" and "Do you remember putting the wind up us by letting go of everything in mid-air and waving 'all fours' at the same time?" I must hasten to add that it was no intention of mine to put the wind up my pupils by waving my arms and legs in the air. I think Redpath must have been referring to my efforts to get my circulation going during long, bitterly cold spells in a box-kite. Those who had to instruct on Tiger Moths in this last war know how cold it can be in a open cockpit. Let them imagine then what it must have been like sitting up in a box-kite like a coachman, with no windscreen at all.

Besides the Americans and Canadians, we had a pupil from Newfoundland – Flight Sub-Lieut. H.V. Reid. He came to us early in 1915 and was the first war pilot from over there. Both his brother and his sister – later the wife of Mr. Alan Butler, aviator and chairman of De Havilland Aircraft – became flyers.

In addition to instructing at Chingford I was, as I mentioned before, also responsible for a great deal of testing. In collaboration with Major C.R. Abbott – a 1911 Brooklands pilot and Admiralty officer in charge of aircraft transportation – I tested and reported on many new machines before he passed them for service overseas. Few pilots will remember the French Horace "Shorthorn" pushers. Only a sprinkling arrived in this country, and, after I had had a near squeak on one, they were scrapped. After climbing up to 5,000 feet with an assistant in one of these Horaces I throttled down to make the descent. To drop through a gap in the clouds, I pushed the nose down into a vertical dive, but, when I pulled the stick back to come out of the dive, there was no response. Though the rudder and lateral controls were working, the elevator was completely non-effective. I hurriedly looked round for a possible clue to the trouble and finally, in a desperate effort, opened the throttle wide to increase the airflow over the elevators. To my intense relief, although we nearly pulled the wings off, it worked. Thank heavens we had the height when the trouble started, for, by the time we came out of that dive, we only had a few hundred feet left between us and the ground.

Though many stories have been told about my defective vision, it really was not as bad as some people thought. I admit I once mistook an Admiralty official carrying two attaché cases for a mechanic bringing a couple of cans of petrol long after I had called for them, and it was unfortunate that my outbursts of rather strong language should have fallen on the wrong ears. Capt. C. Vaughan, another Chingford pupil, reminded me of this incident only a short time ago – but with another one which tended to show my vision in a better light. One day, when the aerodrome was covered with snow, I went up for a test flight. As I circled above I noticed two figures running to the centre of the aerodrome, where they started to make signs in the snow. When they had finished I had no difficulty in deciphering the signs as the words "Right wheel off." Acting on this information, I landed the machine on the left wheel, ruddering at the same time to throw the weight on that side, and finished my landing run something like a top ending its spin. My machine, except for its lost wheel, was undamaged. So, my eyesight was not so bad after all.

Notwithstanding all its other activities, Chingford managed to produce an amusing and interesting fortnightly magazine called *Chingflier*. It was edited by its founder, C.M. Wightman, and sub-editor H. Bingham, assisted by W.M. Connah as secretary. C.G. Grey of *The Aeroplane*, wrote a special article for the first edition, which appeared on October 28th 1916. In it he gave high praise to the skill of British pilots, "who were flying under almost incredible conditions in all parts of the world". Bearing out what I have already written about pilots trained on small aerodromes like Brooklands, "C.G." also wrote: "British aerodromes have much to do with the skill of the pilots. The man who can land with certainty at Brooklands or Chingford, or some of the other British aerodromes, may be considered as knowing something about his job, and he would never have learned as much if he had been trained over the vast, uninterrupted plains of France or Germany."

Writing of the "Shorthorns" reminds me of another of my early war-time pupils, now alas dead for many years, but whose splendid achievements in the First World War before he was killed cannot be too often recorded. He was Major R.S. Dallas, D.S.O., D.S.C., and the following is an extract from an account I have kept, written by a noted Australian air journalist, Major F.A. de V. Robertson, shortly after Dallas was killed:

> He is believed to have accounted for 50 enemy aircraft. He was a magnificent pilot and a most daring scientific air fighter. This was the time of the last general German advance against the 5th Army, and on April 14th 1918 Major Dallas, with three Captains (an unusual formation for a special piece of work), reconnoitred the junction of the First and Second Armies, where the situation was obscure. Early in the mission the Major was wounded by machine-gun fire from the ground (the weather was bad, and the S.E.5s were flying low), but he carried on until he was wounded a second time, when he successfully regained his aerodrome. He seems to have made light of his wounds, for on May 2nd he dropped a boobytrap on a German aerodrome in the form of a parcel marked – "If you won't come up here and fight, herewith one pair of boots for work on the ground – Pilots, for the use of." He then hid in the mist until Germans collected round the parcel, when he attacked them with bombs and machine guns. Major

Dallas was fighting with three triplanes when he was shot down dead. His promotion to Wing Commander did not reach him in time before he was killed.

Shortly after Morgan's death in a "Longhorn" I myself crashed in a Grahame-White (le Rhône engine) with Flight Officer Lavigne, a French-Canadian pupil. Not many seconds after we had taken off my engine began to splutter. The only thing I could do was to go straight ahead into a field with ditches across it. As we touched down, the skids of the machine stuck in the bank of a ditch, and we somersaulted (Figure 36). This time we were both strapped in, and, as we hung upside down, I was beginning to congratulate myself that we had escaped injury, but, on receiving no reply from Lavigne, my feelings changed to acute apprehension. I scrambled out and released him – only to find that he had broken his neck and was dead. Although the subsequent Court of Inquiry exonerated me it could not allay the mental torture I went through. I felt, as I have always felt about my pupils, that we were all one of the same family and Lavigne's death affected me as if he had been a younger brother.

I was rather surprised soon after this accident to be called to London for a medical board and, particularly, an eye test. It was unfortunate, perhaps, that the specialist who tested my eyes was none other than the one who had turned me down before my commission was granted. On leaving him I was sent straight to Sir Godfrey Paine, then Director of Naval Air Services, and was told that I would have to stop flying. With Sir Godfrey's help I was allowed to go before another medical board, this time armed with a civilian specialist's report that my eyes were probably better now than six years before – but all to no avail. The Navy's standard of eyesight has always been high, and the medical officer was adhering strictly to the regulations. Sir Godfrey told me how sorry he was, both for the R.N.A.S. and me, that my flying had been stopped. Encouraged by his kind words, I made up my mind that I would find some way of getting past the eye test. I then returned to Chingford, where I was given a farewell dinner by Commander Ward and the staff at which everyone deplored the fact that I had been grounded.

And so, with wings now clipped, I cast my memory back and reflected on my six eventful flying years. From the time I had started as an instructor until the day I was grounded I had trained nearly

900 pupils, and I was proud in the knowledge that Chingford, like the Bristol School at Brooklands before it, had achieved a reputation second to none in the production of first-class pilots. Comforted by these reflections, I looked round with new hope to see what the future would bring.

Chapter 16

Airborne Again

It was expected that I would be sent for ground duty to Cattewater, a sea-plane station where anti-submarine patrols were being carried out, but by some mistake I was posted instead as a senior Intelligence Officer to Manston. Although Manston was also a patrol station and was frequently raided by enemy bombers, it was considered a good training ground for young Flight Officers before they went on to France. In the short time I was there, though officially grounded, I went up at the request of Flight-Lieut. Lord Ossulston as his "passenger" to give him some "dual". He had been taught to fly by Flight-Lieut. A.B. Watkins, one of my earlier pupils, and wanted a few tips on instructional work. Some years later he wrote to me saying he had never forgotten that thirty-minute flight in the Avro. "In that short trip," he wrote, "I learned more from you about the gentle art of flying than in many previous hours in the air."

I was only at Manston a week before it was discovered, as I had suspected, that there had been a mistake in my posting, and I was transferred to Cattewater. Capt. West was in command, and a Chingford pupil, Flight Commander K. Buss, was on the staff. Here I was surprised to hear from a number of pupils and pilots who had been sent to Calshot on special courses that the sea-planes were heavy to handle and, in some instances, almost without "feel". Hearing this, I thought that Lance Sieveking's description of the Nieuport monoplane sea-planes as "flying omnibuses" was particularly appropriate.

Terribly envious of the pilots around me, I nevertheless did my best to accustom myself to my new status and was much helped by finding that I had a complete friend in Capt. West. It was he who told me to have patience while he thought out a way "of smuggling me back to flying". Through his influence I was once more medically examined, this time at the R.N. Hospital, Devonport. The eye specialist here told me that, while my direct visual acuity was below normal, my peripheral vision was good. He thought that my fitness for instructional duty should be decided by those capable of judging my past record and should not be unduly prejudiced by ophthalmic opinion alone, and he ended by saying: "I should not hesitate to trust myself to your care as far as visual acuity is concerned." On this Capt. West submitted that I should be reappointed as a Flying Instructor. Eventually, by dint of much pulling and pushing in higher circles, we extracted an official notification that I would be permitted to make a trial solo flight at Cattewater, after which a decision would be made by the Admiralty.

Before I embark on the tale of this trial flight I must explain that I had never flown a sea-plane and that by this time I had been off flying for four months. When I look back, it all seems very amusing; but at the time it was anything but. When the day came I boarded a 130 h.p. single-seater Baby Hamble Scout and was duly lowered by crane on to the water (Figure 37), where I started the engine with the handle inside the cockpit and taxied out. Everything depended on this flight, and, so anxious was I to make a good impression, that I made the cardinal error of omitting to secure the starting-handle. Noticing that there was a large vessel with a tall mast in front of me, I pointed the nose to one side, opened the throttle smoothly and began my take-off. The difference between land and sea-planes in taking off was immediately obvious. The ruffled surface of the water made it more difficult, and the whole feeling was far sloppier. As we became airborne I saw that I had not allowed the ship enough room, and, if I had not gone into an immediate vertical bank, I should have hit the mast with my right wing-tip. "Come on Merriam," I muttered, and, then, having recovered from this temporary set-back, I proceeded to climb. Shock number two came when I went to flatten out. The stick would not go forward. A quick look down and there was that blank starting-handle which I had forgotten to secure jamming the forward movement of the stick. There was only one way out of it – to pull the stick right back and risk stalling the machine to release the handle. To do this I had to undo my safety-belt, whip back the stick, and then bend down, disengage the handle and push the stick forward before the Scout had time to stall. With my heart in my mouth, I managed it successfully. Without worrying about my loose belt, I now settled down to some real flying. For the next ten minutes I proceeded to put the machine through her paces, finishing up by cutting out the engine at 2,000 feet and landing just in front of the spot from where I had taken off.

Everyone thought I had done remarkably well, but I had difficulty in keeping a straight face when someone remarked on the "cute" stunts I had performed after taking off.

I carried out two more flights, and eventually a message was received from the Admiralty that I was to be allowed to resume my flying duties. To my joy, I found that I was not to go back to instructing only, but would be taking part in anti-submarine patrols and testing as well as exercising general supervision over some of the Cattewater flying. Operations from Cattewater consisted almost entirely of anti-submarine patrolling in Short sea-planes fitted with wireless, bombs and room for an observer, Schneider (Sopwith) Scouts and Baby Hamble Scouts. The Scouts carried a couple of 65-lb. bombs, but they were so tricky to land, particularly when there was any sort of sea running, that only Flight Commander Buckland and I used them.

My first few patrols were uneventful, and it was not until my seventh patrol, on September 29th 1917, that I had my first taste of action. Our orders at that time were to bomb at sight every submarine wherever encountered except in certain areas where our own submarines were operating; but, even in these areas, a submarine that started to dive after a recognition signal had been given was to be attacked instantly. September 29th was a rough day with a fairly heavy, white-horse sea. The U-boats liked this sort of weather because it was difficult for the destroyers escorting the convoys to see their periscopes until they were in firing range. Visibility was good, and I was playing hide and seek in the puff-ball-like clouds at about 5,000 feet when I saw a lone merchantman majestically ploughing her way towards Plymouth. I decided to have a closer look at her and started to spiral down with my engine off. As I popped out of the clouds and searched round to see if there were any more ships in sight, I spotted what looked like a submarine on the surface about a quarter of a mile to one side of the merchantman. It was pointing straight at her. I continued to descend and prepared to attack. "What luck", I thought, I decided to glide down. "They haven't noticed me." But, although I was pretty sure I could not be heard as long as I did not open up my engine, the noise of the wind whistling past the fuselage seemed deafening. At 1,500 feet I could see it was definitely a U-boat, and, at the same time, I saw two figures in the conning tower suddenly rush below. They had seen me! Diving steeply while I fused my bombs, I dropped the first lot smack on top of the conning tower just as it was submerging and released the second lot so that they would fall just in front of the submarine. I am absolutely certain I sank it. After the upheaval from the explosions had subsided I saw a considerable amount of debris floating about and a large pool of oil. My petrol being low, I circled round long enough only to make sure the merchantman was clear of immediate danger and then returned to base. After reporting my "kill" I refuelled, rearmed and set out again to patrol the area, but saw no further signs. So thrilled was I by my success that I carried out two more patrols that day and nearly attacked one of our own motor launches, which, from a height, seemed to me uncommonly like a submarine!

It was while operating on these patrols that I came across an unusual form of alleged "air-sickness". The medical officer had asked me to take one or two of the pilots up and to submit a report on them. I came to the conclusion that the complaint was not "air sickness" but "sea fright" and was in most instances experienced after a forced descent at sea. Patrols miles out from the land were a severe strain on the nerves of men who knew that their machines could stand little buffeting from the waves should they be forced to come down. Pilots who had to make long flights over the sea or jungle in single-engine machines during this last war and knew they would stand a very poor chance if their engines cut out, have told me they experienced a similar feeling of hopelessness. It was an infectious feeling, and it was soon possible for a couple of pilots to pass it on to the rest of the squadron. During my instructional career I had seen many accidents and had been able to judge the cause of quite a few of them, but the non-return of a pilot and machine from a sea patrol I found uncanny. Rarely did you learn why they had not returned, and, unless you took a firm grip on your imagination, it was very easy to become jumpy.

The submarine menace had become so grave in 1917 that nearly all the Service aircraft in Britain were being used in helping the destroyers and torpedo boats to protect our convoys. From the air, to watch these convoys zigzagging, even though you knew they were still in some danger, was a beautiful and fascinating sight. One day, on my return from a deviation towards Dartmouth, I actually saw a merchantman sinking off Start Point. The crew were taking to their boats, and, about half a mile to one side, I could see a disturbance on the water. As I had little fuel to spare, I dropped a bomb on the disturbed water and flew to signal the nearest coastguard station. When I arrived back I signalled the men in the boats that they were under observation and, after circling round a few minutes, dropped my other bomb near the first and turned towards base. My anxiety for the safety of the merchant sailors had caused me to stay out longer than I should have. When still four miles from Plymouth my engine cut out through lack of fuel, and I had to make a forced landing on the choppy sea. After I had spent some hours rocking about and had fired all but my last "Very" Light I was spotted by a Short seaplane returning from patrol. A small fishing smack then came to my assistance, and this I hung on to until the arrival of a tug to tow me to Cattewater. Several times during my wait I slipped from the floats of the sea-plane into the water, becoming each time more numbed by the cold, November sea.

"All's well that ends well." When I finally reached base with my machine fortunately still undamaged, I was relieved to hear that the crew of the merchantman had all been rescued.

Chapter 17

Down in the Drink

We soon discovered that the U-boats hated aircraft because they knew they could be so easily spotted by them. Very few submarines were destroyed by aircraft, but, if the U-boats knew they were in areas we could patrol, they went very warily, and when the Admiralty awoke to the full importance of air cover they found that where air cover was supplied, convoys were seldom molested. But it took some time to reach this stage, and it was only just before the end of the First World War that two ships were adapted for carrying aircraft. Seeing that at one time it was touch and go whether the U-boat campaign might not prove disastrously successful, it is hard to understand why we were so slow in expanding our air arm in this direction. Had it not been for the splendid efforts of our hard-worked destroyers, helped by the Americans' and Britain's trawler fleet, we should never have succeeded in breaking the blockade. And what an expensive method it was to use anything from 200 to 1,000 tons of valuable material on the sea in areas where four or five tons in the air could do the job just as well with far fewer trained men.

In my few months at Cattewater I became convinced, as a result of my own and other pilots' experience of anti-submarine patrols, of the importance of the air arm in this sphere. Most of my patrols were termed "emergency", and I did not have to carry out the long, thankless patrol flights in Short sea-planes, which were so tiring to handle in rough weather. My friends, Flight-Lieut. W.B. Callaway and Flight Sub-Lieuts. H.P.D. Lane and V.R. Scriven, were among those who were mainly tied down to these monotonous missions, and, as there were many ships to protect and few aircraft to do it, they were constantly on the go. Nevertheless, it was a great joy to go out and meet the convoys. And they were just as pleased to see us. You could see the crews waving, and, if you switched off your engine, you could even hear them cheering and the ships hooting.

Every now and then, after returning from a patrol, we would be ordered out again to search for a lost aircraft. More often than not, it was a fruitless task. Even in good weather, few planes could remain for long on the water, and, if the seas were heavy, they were soon battered to pieces and sunk. I had often imagined the torture of mind of pilots and observers forced down on the sea far from land, but, when my turn came, I found that imagination, for once, fell woefully short of the real thing.

As the result of information that U-boats had been seen forty miles from Start Point, I was hastily ordered to proceed with the utmost dispatch on an emergency patrol in that area. Full of excitement I ran out to my Scout, saying to myself as I went – "Chance for another one, Merriam." Arrived over the area, I started a careful search but could see no sign of U-boats or, indeed, of any other craft. I was just beginning to curse my luck in having been sent on another fruitless errand when my engine began to splutter. Dismay was hardly the word for my feelings. I was forty miles from the land, there wasn't a floating object in sight, and, worse still, I had been in such a hurry to get airborne that I had forgotten my life-belt. "If you ever get out of this, Merriam, you'll never leave the deck without at least two life-belts and a pair of water-wings", I swore as I set course for the nearest land. The engine steadily deteriorated, spluttering, stopping for short periods and then bursting into life again to give me new hope, but only to splutter to a stop after a few seconds. It was obviously fuel starvation, but the knowledge did not make me any happier. All this time I was losing height. The engine would stop, I would depress the nose to glide, and it would start again. Then, I would pull the nose up, and it would stop once more. Each time we got lower and lower, and the waves got nearer and nearer. When the engine picked up I tried flying level. Though this kept it running for a few seconds longer, it was obvious we were not going to remain airborne for long. Finally the engine cut out altogether, and, turning into wind, I put the Scout down on top of a roller, tail down.

The waves were bigger than I had expected. They were six-feet high and promised to give my frail craft slight chance of surviving for long, and, as I sent up a couple of "Very" Lights in the hope that something might be in the neighbourhood, a huge roller engulfed us. From the rear of the plane there came an ominous cracking sound, and, as I struggled out of the cockpit on to the floats, I could see she had broken her back. I moved forward on the floats to keep the tail up and began to feel my hands becoming numb in the bitter December cold. Knowing that, if I lost my grip and slipped into the water I would never be able to struggle back again, I lashed myself to the float-struts with my coat belt and a piece of old strapping from my pocket. Each succeeding wave seemed as if it would devour us. Several times my feet were forced from the float and I was suspended knee deep in the water. What a mercy I was tied on! As each wave approached I twined my legs more firmly round the struts and felt so physically fatigued that I almost forgot my mental torture. I knew that only one chance in a thousand would save me. I learned afterwards that I must have been hanging on for three and a half hours when my signals were at last spotted.

It must have been then that I looked wearily up and thought I could see smoke on the horizon. I was so exhausted that it is still a mystery to me how I managed to raise my pistol and fire one of my last two distress signals, and even then I dared not hope my signal had been seen. The smoke appeared to be stationary, and an eternity seemed to pass while I gazed at it in suspense. In desperation I summoned up all my courage and fired my last remaining "Very" Light. After another agonizing suspense I began to recognize the outlines of a destroyer. A little later and to my immense joy I dimly discerned that a boat was being rowed towards me. A few minutes after I was being pulled into safety and remembered nothing more until I found myself wrapped in warm blankets in a bunk.

When I was sufficiently recovered the Commander told me that my last signal was the only one they had seen. It had been a near thing. Thinking I might have been shot down by a U-boat, they had dropped depth charges all round. I had become so exhausted that I had not noticed the explosions. He also told me that, while I had been resting, a Short sea-plane had flown over them and – probably seeing the wreckage of my Scout suspended on the side of the destroyer – had signalled: "Have you pilot Merriam aboard?"

The joy of that evening in the destroyer! Officers and men made me feel thoroughly at home, and, even when we nearly collided at full speed in the dark with another ship, I remained happy and unperturbed.

To land me, the Commander decided to put in earlier than scheduled, but, through some mistake in the code, we were ordered to retire immediately or be fired on, and we had to cruise about for a further hour until, after a long exchange of signals, we were eventually allowed to enter harbour.

It was a great relief to be back at base, where I was treated at first like a man returned from the dead. Horrible though my experience had been, it did teach me two or three valuable lessons. From it I learnt the importance of landing dead into the wind, setting the plane down in a squatting position and of putting her on top of a wave. I am certain that had I missed that wave and not put my machine down tail first, my frail Scout would have broken up right away.

As I was afraid of getting into the hands of the doctors again and being put through another eyesight test I insisted on returning to work after only twenty-four hours' rest. Two days later I was testing again and within a few days I was back on patrols. But, after the first long patrol, I realized that my nerves were still frayed. Each time I got out over the sea I was a prey to a desolating feeling of loneliness and haunted by the fear of more engine trouble. For this reason I was grateful when I was switched to ferrying sea-planes and flying-boats for a while, though, even with them, frequent forced descents from engine failure imposed a heavy strain on my nerves.

There is no doubt that at this late stage of the war our aero engines were becoming less and less reliable. Air Commodore C.W.H. Pulford, a one-time "Chingflier", told me that when he was forming and training the first torpedo squadron in 1918 for a suicide attack on the German High Seas Fleet – fortunately the surrender of the Fleet made this attack unnecessary – his pilots' chief worry was about their engines. Marcus Manton, too, who was then testing at Samuel Whites, told me that not only was he experiencing a lot of trouble with engines, but that Calshot was having a number of serious crashes through the same cause. When a pilot like Manton began to complain, you could be sure there was good reason, for he was at that time one of the foremost test pilots in the country. It looked as if in the enormous speed-up of production now achieved that quality was being sacrificed to quantity. Of course, pilots and air crews welcomed more aircraft and engines, but they certainly did not want them at the expense of reliability.

I was flying one day with Sub-Lieut. Lane in a Norman Thompson flying-boat when we were forced down near Torquay. It was rather late in the day when the rescue launch arrived to tow us to Dartmouth, and before we were moored alongside the carrier, H.M.S. "Reveria" night had already fallen. That night I slept in the carrier. The next morning when I took off it was so misty that I did not see the cliffs ahead and had not realized that the "Reveria" was moored so close to the land. It was only by doing a vertical bank immediately I was airborne that I escaped crashing into them, and it was a matter of inches whether my top wing hit the cliffs or my lower one the water. In my later flights when low over the sea in misty conditions near the Devon and Cornish coast I found that visibility was most deceptive. The mist seemed to cling to the cliffs from their base upwards and form a thick curtain which looked no more than a low cloud through which one could fly at will.

Chapter 18

A Word About Blimps

In March 1918, I was posted to the R.N.A.S. Station at Mullion, in Cornwall, for a spell of aerial photography and coastal mapping. Here we used land machines. They were the famous 110-130 h.p. Sopwith 1½ Strutters (Figure 40) which had done such excellent work as fighters on the Somme in the late summer and autumn of 1916 and were so named on account of their unusual centre section struts. Though since superseded as fighters they were still useful outside the main battle zone. In them we made mapping flights at 10,000 feet and photographed the Cornish coast to make sure our fortifications were adequately camouflaged.

Except for these Sopwiths, all the aircraft at Mullion were small airships known as "Blimps". These Blimps were a mongrel type of machine, being little more than the fuselage of an aeroplane suspended below a sausage-shaped gas bag (Figure 41). They did most useful anti-submarine work and would have been ideal for that purpose in those days if they had possessed sufficient engine power and speed to stand up to rough weather. As it was, they were only fair-weather "birds". In the absence of the long-range air fighters which the Germans later developed to such effect against our convoys and air escorts in the Second World War the "Blimps" had little to fear from enemy action as long as they operated only at a fair distance from hostile territory. In spite of their weather limitations they did have certain definite advantages over aeroplanes. They could, for one thing, remain in the air a considerable time – a very useful characteristic when searching a suspected submarine area, and, for another, they could and often did effect an almost complete engine overhaul while in the air.

When I was at Cattewater I had made a few trips in the kite balloons which were attached to destroyers for observation purposes, but, like most other aeroplane pilots, I found little to interest me in any lighter-than-air machine. Although two of their Flight Commanders took a spot of tuition with me in a plane and seemed to enjoy it, heavier-than-air machines appeared to be equally unpopular with airship pilots.

While, as I have confessed, I had no liking for "Blimps" or airships, I think it is only fair to pause a moment in my story to make a brief mention of the valuable work they did during the First World War. German submarine commanders admitted they feared the airships more than the aeroplanes because they could stay out longer over the danger areas and were so often about at night when the submarines surfaced. In the danger areas, too, the airships stuck so close to their convoys that the U-boats found it very difficult to attack without being spotted. Some idea of the efficiency of the airship patrols can be gathered from the record of one of the most distinguished airship pilots, Squadron Leader York-Moore. During his time he escorted 800 ships without a single one being attacked, and from mid-1915 to November 1918 his total hours on escort duty came to about 2,000. On his last flight he took his airship from Kingsnorth to Stamford Bridge to take cinematograph pictures of an international rugby match from inside the ground at a height of only twenty feet. Mullion airship station was well known through the Service for its extraordinarily high record. Many thousands of ships, including the coal convoys from Penzance to Brest, were safely escorted by Mullion men through that part of the Western approaches. The importance of these airship operations and of the great part Mullion took in them can be gauged by the fact that no less than four D.S.C.s, three D.S.M.s and nine "mentions" were awarded to Mullion airship officers and men.

About this time I put in for and was granted some much-needed leave. Before departing, however, I met with an experience of a type I had so often met before and of no great interest in itself, but which leads me to relate the experience of another man which began like mine but ended in a very different fashion. On returning from a photographic flight I found the air station and its surroundings practically blotted out by a sea mist. I came down to fifty feet and could just make out the outline of the huge airship hangar. Judging it too risky to attempt a landing there, I flew on and eventually managed to get down in a small field near Falmouth. The Commanding Officer and one of his Squadron Leaders, I learned later, were both watching and thought I was going to crash into the wireless masts. Flight Commander E.A. de Ville, one of my Chingford pupils, under similar conditions at Portsmouth, not only crashed into a wireless mast but remained perched in his machine on its very tall top, and there he had to stop until a sailor climbed up to his assistance!

When I returned to duty after my leave I found that I had been posted as second-in-command of No. 250 Squadron at Padstow, another anti-submarine station. This time the machines were all land planes – D.H.6s, D.H.9s, and 90 h.p. Curtiss's. Their engines were more reliable for sea patrols than those of the sea-planes, and take-offs, landings and maintenance were much easier. On reporting at Padstow I found that the R.N.A.S. and the R.F.C. had been amalgamated to form the New Royal Air Force and that our Commanding Officer was Major R.E. Orton from the R.F.C. Orton was a most pleasant man to work under. It was particularly fortunate at this juncture, because the inevitable friction aroused by the sudden fusion of two Services with different ideas and tactics called for the most tactful and sympathetic handling.

Most of my time at Padstow was spent in testing and experimenting with heavier bomb loads and taking part in patrols, but I also helped with the instructing of several young R.F.C. officers. While I was there my son Olin, who had joined the Sea Scouts and was helping the coast watching patrols, came to stay with me. I occasionally took him for flights and used him to help with messenger and coastal observation work. It was during his visit that one of the scouts fell over the high cliffs into the water. He managed to scramble on to a rock and was rescued some hours later by Petty Officer Burt and Private Keane of Padstow Coastguard Station after they had made a 270 feet cliff descent by ropes at night.

Among the first-class pilots at Padstow were Capt. Wadham and Talbot-Lehmann and Lieut. Scott, A.E.N. Ashford, A.H. Blundell and V.A.F. Rolandi, but probably the best remembered man there was the medical officer, G.M. Mellor. He was a jovial personality and amused us a lot by starting a craze for close-cropped hair. Led by him, we were all induced to have our heads cropped like convicts, with results that caused several of our visitors to wonder if they had mistaken their destination and come to a prison instead of an air station. When I took Mellor up for his first flight nearly all the station turned out to watch. He quite frankly admitted that he disliked the idea intensely, but that every time he went on leave people, seeing his uniform, thought he was a flying man. Rather than disillusion them or wander from the realms of truth, he had decided to brave our element. I certainly admired his frankness, but could not repress a quiet smile at the sight of his "Dutch courage" bulging from his pocket as he climbed into the cockpit.

Another interesting character was our Adjutant, Lieut. F.H. Reynolds. He was a popular officer who had earlier been wounded and had lost the use of his left hand. It was not until after the Armistice that I learnt he had also been a missionary and had travelled all over the world before the war.

A welcome visitor to Padstow at this time was the late Air Vice-Marshal F.V. Holt. It was our first meeting for six years, the last being when I had taught him to fly in 1912. Unfortunately, it turned out that it was the last time I was to see him alive.

Engine trouble was not always the curse we feared. It was due to engine trouble that I had a visit from another 1912 pilot, Colonel J.T. Babington. We had not met since the days when I used to test machines at Eastchurch. A final memorable visit was the one we received while I was acting squadron commander from General Mark Kerr, who had been taught to fly in Greece by none other than my old friend, Collyns Pizey. He came to inspect the squadron and, I am glad to say, was very complimentary.

The terrible influenza epidemic which swept the country soon after the Armistice took its full toll from Padstow. I was one of its victims and was in bed recovering from the attack when a message was handed to me from Brigadier-General H.P. Smyth Osbourne informing me that I had been awarded the Air Force Cross. This news was the finest tonic I could have. By this time I had flown over 5,000 hours according to my log-book, piloted nearly sixty different types of aircraft and taught just on a thousand pupils. I received many letters of congratulation, one of the most treasured coming from Major Gilbert More of the U.S. naval forces operating in European waters.

Just before the Armistice I had been recommended to succeed Major Orton as C.O. of the squadron. When it came I was transferred almost at once for instructional duty to the 29th Training Squadron at Croydon. My pupils were released prisoners of war, and I remained there until my demobilization in May 1919. My posting to Croydon was the work of Lieut.-Col. G.F. Pretyman, an old Brooklands' pupil who was then on the training staff. Pretyman told me that he only wished I could have arrived a week earlier, because he would then have recommended me as instructor to the Duke of York (later King George VI). I was naturally very disappointed. As Pretyman said, the name of the second in succession to the Throne would have been a deserved and appropriate addition to my long list of notable pupils.

After about three months' instructing I was laid low for some weeks by an acute attack of that rheumatic gout which so frequently afflicted pilots, and was shortly afterwards discharged from the R.A.F. with the rank of Captain (late Flight Commander, R.N.). About the same time I heard, like many others, that my application for a permanent commission had been unsuccessful.

Chapter 19

Sea-Plane Joy Flights

Disappointed at having been turned down by the Service I had grown to love, and wondering doubtfully what civilian life had to offer me, my interest and hopes were suddenly aroused by the *Daily Mail*'s announcement of the handsome prize it would award to the first person to fly the Atlantic. Hearing that Grahame-White was entering a machine, I offered to fly it. He, however, soon withdrew his entry, and I then applied to Commander Perrin, Secretary of the Royal Aero Club, who had been authorized to accept competitors' names. At this time many firms had already made their entries and engaged their pilots, among the latter being Harry Hawker, F.P. Raynham, Major H.G. Brackley and Capt. A. Payze. But I heard that Vickers still wanted a pilot and that I stood a good chance. At a casual meeting in the Royal Aero Club I mentioned this to Jack Alcock. He had just returned from a long period as prisoner of war in Turkey and was himself keen to get a machine to fly in the *Daily Mail* competition. After some friendly discussion we eventually decided to toss up for which of us was to apply to Vickers. Jack won the toss and was accepted. It is now a matter of world history that he and his navigator, Whitten-Brown, were the first ever to fly across the Atlantic, which they did in 16 hours 12 minutes – a magnificent flight and one for which they were deservedly knighted. Alcock's death six months later while landing in a fog in France came as a shock to the nation and was a personal loss to me.

I now began to think of applying for a commercial aviation licence, but, feeling no longer fit for lengthy bouts of strenuous flying, I was doubtful if I could manage to pass the necessary medical tests.

However, I did pass them and within a few weeks was engaged to work under Lieut.-Col. G.O.P. Henderson, M.C., A.F.C., in the organization of a joy-riding project at various towns and seaside resorts, the scheme being under the general direction of Mr. E.V. Roe, brother of the celebrated "A. V."

Sea-plane flights proved to be very popular with the post-war public (Figures 42 and 43). I kept a motor-boat as a tender and a sea-plane which was moored each night in the Medina River off Cowes. Two passengers at a time were taken up, and our charges ranged from one guinea upwards for a seven- to ten-minute flight. I was assisted by a mechanic and a booking clerk. During fine spells of weather we were kept very busy, and, if we had had more planes and pilots, we should have made a great deal of money. On a single machine I found the overheads were heavy. Moreover, the deterioration of floats and fabric through the action of sea water was more rapid than we had anticipated, and the fuel consumption of an engine in a sea-plane was heavier than that of the same engine in a land plane. However, after two months of hard work with no mishaps, I was able to pay salaries, mooring fees, launch expenses – in fact, all overheads – and still show a substantial profit.

Sandown in the Isle of Wight was by far the best resort to work from. While we were there visitors from Shanklin, Ventnor and every part of the island flocked in regularly for flights. Strangely enough, most of my passengers were women, the elderly matrons being just as enthusiastic as the young flappers but not always as profitable. Weight was a matter of some importance. Our machine was so low powered that it could not take more than twenty stone in addition to the pilot. If a passenger weighed much over ten stone, I had to make a special flight with that passenger alone. One determined woman, weighing, I imagine, quite eighteen stone, was so cumbersome that she fell head first into the cockpit in her keenness to get aboard. By the time we had righted her and settled her in, much of our costly fuel had been wasted. We soon learnt that overweights actually lose us money and that we must refuse them unless they were prepared to pay double fare. Explaining this, I found, though it always raised a laugh among the onlookers, was apt to be resented by the heavier visitors. But there was one exception. Mr. Thomas, a popular Sandown business personality, used to come up for regular trips, and, as he was very heavy, he insisted on paying double fare each time.

Incidents were rare, but I remember one that occurred after I had agreed to take a married couple back to Cowes one evening on the man's assurance that he was a keen yachtsman and could help me moor the plane. This meant leaving my mechanic, who usually went back with me. Deciding, after we had alighted on the Medina, that it would be inadvisable – in case he should be hit by the propeller – to let the yachtsman go out on the floats, I stepped on to them myself and grabbed the mooring buoy. There was a strong tide running, and, before I realized what was happening, the sea-plane was simply swept away from under my feet and I was left hanging on to the buoy in mid-stream. I swam after the machine as though the devil were behind me, struggled aboard and was just in time to start the engine and avert a collision with a barge. My male passenger, I am thankful to say, had had the presence of mind to step out on to the floats to pull me in.

By the end of the season I came to the conclusion I had had enough of joy flights, and, thinking it would make a happy temporary break, I started chicken farming. I was not the first and am certainly not the last to think that life on a chicken farm would spell happiness. I soon found that my temperament was quite unsuited to playing head cook and bottlewasher to a crowd of featherbrains, and I was delighted to find an excuse to leave it for a while when Mr. S.E. Saunders asked me to test an experimental amphibian plane called "Kittiwake" (Figure 44). This machine was constructed almost entirely of Consuta plywood, which was sewn together by machinery like ordinary canvas. It was Mr. Saunders' own idea and was fitted with two 250 h.p. A.B.C. engines. Two or three previous attempts by test pilots had succeeded in getting Kittiwake only a few feet off the water and then not without damaging her. Quite wrongly, in my opinion, she had been given a bad name, and Mr. Saunders had not been able up to date to find another pilot with experience to put her through her paces. He was convinced she was a sound machine and had put a lot of money into her. Much to the delight of Mr. Saunders, P.H. Beadle, the designer, and Mr. Gravenell, the superintendent constructor, after a series of minor structural alterations and a few hops over the water, I took three passengers in Kittiwake's comfortable and attractively upholstered cabin for a forty-five-minute flight over the Isle of Wight, Calshot and Hamble. But, in spite of this successful flight, Kittiwake was doomed to an early end and to leave no progeny. During my absence on business she was taken up by an Air Ministry pilot and crashed. The pilot claimed she was uncontrollable, which was strange, for I had found her quite pleasant to handle. I still think she was a valuable type that could have been made a success, but, as a great deal of money, which at that time could be ill-afforded, had already been spent on her development, all further work was now abandoned. I have to confess that the A.M.'s pilot had been one of my own pupils.

For these test flights I was paid £1 per flying minute – a handsome sum for those days. I could have made more good money like this when Wing Commander Pretyman introduced me to Juan de la Cierva, the inventor of the famous Autogiro, but, as it meant a great deal more work than my health could then stand, I regretfully had to decline his offer. It was Capt. Frank Courtney who eventually made the tests.

On my return to my farm I added to it pigs, geese, ducks, cows and horses in the hope that they might induce me to take a real interest in farming, for I could see that my health would no longer allow me to keep going at strenuous flying for any length of time.

This hope was fulfilled until the day when the *Daily Mail* announced its Gliding Competition. In a moment I realized that here was a new sphere of aviation in which pioneer work would be needed, and, overnight, my farming became comparatively un-important. Previous to this I had attended a dinner in 1920 to the survivors of the first hundred British aviators and the pioneers of British aviation which was given at the Connaught Rooms in London and was presided over by the Duke of York. The dinner had been the idea of Major C.C. Turner, then editor of *Aeronautics*, and many eminent representatives of the aviation world were present. I was seated at the same table as Wing Commander H. Blackburn, Major W.H. Ewen, Mr. Compton Patterson, M. Louis Noel, Mr. R. Wickham, Mr. Lionel H. Mander, Mr. Fred May, Mr. Scott-Paine, Mr. Frank Fisher, and Major J.H. Ledeboer. The function was a great success, and, when I returned to the farm I was already unconsciously groping for a place in aviation where I could plan an effective part. The announcement of the gliding competition came just at the right time.

Following the announcement, I got in touch with Mr. G. Newman, then works manager of Saunders at East Cowes, and we decided to build our own glider for the competition. Mr. Hodson, Mr. Weaver and one or two others helped us to build it in the Saunders works in the evenings. It was a monoplane type with a wing span of thirty-six feet and had a really wonderful lift (Figure 45). Trial flights on my farm were so encouraging that we were confident of success when we took it to Firle Beacon, near Brighton, for the competition (Figure 48).

Beginners as we were in the art of launching, when the time came we made the mistake of taking off too near the ridge. As I became airborne I found the wind was stronger than the elastic launching catapult, and was beginning to drive me backwards. If the launchers had let go when they saw my predicament, I could have flattened out; but they hung on, and the next moment I came down in a vertical dive, completely out of control (Figure 46). I was lucky to escape from the crash with only a minor injury to my foot. Herr Fokker, the Dutch designer, sportingly offered to lend me his glider. I accepted, but, when I was about to be launched, the mist engulfed us and prevented me from making any further attempts.

Though the *Daily Mail* prize was won by M. Maneyrol, it was Herr Fokker who really showed us that day how to soar. Mr. F. Raynham put up the next best show, but Gordon England crashed and severely injured his leg. The meeting had all the spirit of the early flying days at Brooklands and brought together many of aviation's pioneers, all intent on studying the possibilities of this new sphere. To us there it was already apparent that Germany was making rapid strides in the new art. Forbidden to experiment with powered aircraft after the First World War, she had turned her attention to gliding, with the intention, as we realized later, of building up a potential pilot force for military purposes.

I was convinced that there was also a great future for popular gliding in Britain, and decided straight away to investigate the possibility of starting a gliding school. Surely this was the chance the public and country had been waiting for, the chance to give our youngsters cheap and reasonably safe flying, the chance to make Britain air minded. Powered flying was still beyond the pocket of the average man, but gliding was a sport that could be afforded by any youngster with a little pocket money and initiative.

In due course I was granted an interview with Sir Sefton Brancker, then Director of Civil Aviation, at which I put my idea forward and asked what support I could expect from the Ministry. He assured me I had his complete approval and support and that, furthermore, as soon as I was ready to open my school I could use his name. I estimated to spend close on £1,000 in erecting sheds, preparing the site and on converting my original glider to use for dual instruction. It was the first dual control glider, and the seats were so arranged that it could be flown with or without a passenger. It was also designed so that a small engine could be installed and still leave a good factor of safety.

My project was warmly welcomed by the Press as a venture of national importance, and, when I opened the "Whiteley Bank School of Gliding", it was loudly heralded as England's first gliding school. Eager and confident, I notified Sir Sefton that I was ready to start and suggested that the Air League might send along a number of cadets. In his reply Sir Sefton told me he had forwarded my letter to the Secretary of the Air League, Mr. Douglas Gordon, and also suggested that Lord Trenchard might be able to help. But it seemed from the ominous silence that afterwards followed and the absence of any active interest that my idea had been born too soon. I slowly began to understand that, while there would be plenty of verbal support for my project, there would not be any practical help. Eventually, though I had orders for Merriam-Newman gliders and a number of prospective pupils to start, among whom was Mrs. Maurice Hewlett, the first British woman aviator, I was forced to throw my hand in because I could not afford to run at a loss. It was a bitter disappointment. I had been so sure of support from the powers that be and had been so "boosted" by the Press, that I had not stopped to consider that I might be left to carry on alone. My sole practical supporter revealed himself to be living in Canada. He was a former pupil, Capt. K.F. Saunders, and he wrote, bless him, that he was willing to pack up his own work and join me. It was too late.

After this, two more disasters then descended on me with such rapidity that I was left completely despondent. A fire destroyed my main fowl house and over a hundred pedigree Leghorn pullets, and I discovered that in my preoccupation with gliding I had omitted to insure either the fowl house or the chickens. And then, without warning and just at the time I most needed it, my small disability pension was suddenly reduced. Aided by Sir Murray Sueter, I managed to get my pension restored to its former value, but I had so overtaxed my health with the strain and worry of these happenings that I suffered a complete breakdown and had to go into hospital.

Chapter 20

Birth of the Bureau

While I was in hospital my son, Olin, became critically ill and shortly afterwards died. Then followed the death of my father. For some weeks after these sad events I remained in a state of severe depression, and, finding that under the doctors I was making no improvement, I took matters into my own hands and left the hospital. For the next eight months I lived pretty nearly on the highest points of Ventnor and Brading Downs, breathing in the strong sea air and giving my mind a thorough rest from business worries. At first there seemed to be no improvement, but gradually I found my strength returning and, with it, my former urge to get to work.

What could I do? My medical category would never allow me to obtain a commercial licence again – that I knew. Surely there must still be a place in aviation for me. Slowly a new idea began to develop. With my age and health, a post in the Air Ministry, I knew, was hopeless. Though Sir Murray Sueter and other friends had done their best, it seemed that, despite my years of accumulated experience, no place could be found there for a person like myself. But what about setting up as an independent aeronautical consultant and agent? No one had tried anything like that before, and I felt there was a need for an independent organization which could bridge the gap between the existing branches of aviation and the public. It would be a bureau where, for instance, parents wishing to put their sons or daughters into civil aviation could come for advice, and where pilots, firms and skilled personnel would be so classified and indexed that at a moment's notice it would be possible to provide the right man or the right firm for any job required. I decided to go ahead.

When I had made this decision I heard that Sir Samuel Hoare, then a Secretary of State, was interested and would be glad to help me as far as he could. I also received an assurance from Sir Sefton Brancker that he would do all he could to help but doubted if there was much money to be made out of it. How little he really knew me. It wasn't money I was chiefly after but a chance to play an effective part in the advancement of British aviation. To raise the necessary funds for my project I had to sell most of my property. With this done and with a good send-off from *Flight* and *The Aeroplane*, I launched my bureau in 1926. It soon met with an enthusiastic response, and became a welcome meeting-place for old-timers and several of those whose interest was more recent. Among the former were G. ("Handy") Handasyde and Howard Flanders. Among the latter there were two I particularly remember who have now become well known – F.G. Miles, who not only designed his famous machines but also tested them, and R.L. Preston, then a young guardsman who was keen on flying light planes, now a Colonel with a C.B.E. and Secretary of the Royal Aero Club.

Early in 1927 I was being assisted in the bureau by Capt. C. Vaughan, a first-class pilot and a pupil of mine in 1915. Together, we conceived the idea of establishing the first sea-plane school at Cowes and of coupling with it land-plane instruction, gliding, air-taxi work and joy riding. Our scheme also included ground lectures on various branches of aviation and even a special course for youngsters intending to take up flying as a career. Heads of schools in the Isle of Wight were enthusiastic about my suggestions for pre-vocational training. In addition to my own Avro land plane, which was already at West Cowes, I obtained an aircraft engine for instructional purposes. Mr. S.E. Saunders granted me free use of the aerodrome at West Cowes, mooring rights in the Medina River for sea-planes and the use of the sheds on the aerodrome. I had already obtained foreshore rights at Sandown and Seaview and was negotiating for others at Bournemouth and Southsea. Our scheme obviously needed financial support, and there again I was encouraged to believe it would be forthcoming by *Flight*'s enthusiasm and its description of the scheme as one – "approved by many of the big people in the aviation world". So it was, but approval is one thing and financial support another. Once again, after having been slapped on the back and cheered on my way, I found myself gently trotting along ahead with the cheers fading away behind me.

With Capt. Vaughan and a ground engineer lent me by Mr. Saunders, I started joy rides on the land plane just before Whitsun, 1928, but, as Vaughan was very busy with me at the London bureau, I soon had to employ a young pilot. Fresh out of the Service and knowing little of the hardships of civilian life, he was not a success. He didn't like soiling his hands or even helping to push the aeroplane out of the sheds; so it was not long before we parted.

In due course the joy-riding boom passed, and, as I found it difficult to keep the islanders interested in flying – it was only the trippers who went for joy rides, I decided to sell my machine and temporarily abandon the school. Once again my idea had come too soon. But my former idea, that of a gliding school, was now beginning to receive more public attention. Germany's outstanding success in this sphere was now making itself felt. I was therefore delighted when Mr. Stanhope Sprigg, editor of *Airways* and *Who's Who in British Aviation*, asked me to write an article on gliding for the former journal. In it I pointed out the value of gliding for pre-power training, its comparative cheapness and safety and the numerous spots where gliding clubs could be formed. I mentioned that it was six years since the *Daily Mail* competition at Itford Hill and deplored the fact that nothing had been done to foster gliding since then. "Gliders" I concluded, "are being almost entirely neglected in favour of power-driven aircraft, with the result that we are in danger of losing the interest of thousands of potential young aviators." About this time I also contributed an article to *Airways* advocating a proper system of training for entrants to the "Merchant Navy" of the air.

I notice that Charles Gardner, formerly B.B.C. air correspondent, in a series of recent talks round the country has also been stressing this point about civil training. Civil flying has little in common with military flying, and more should be done to train pilots from the start for commercial careers. I was preaching this in those days of 1928. I felt then, as I do to a less extent now, that valuable experience was being lost to the country by the haphazard way in which we were carrying on aviation. The R.A.F. was efficient enough for its own purpose, but it was training men for a fighting service in which machines were built principally for war performance and safety for pilots or their craft was not as important as in civil flying. Much of this has now changed, and the R.A.F. of today certainly places more emphasis on safety in its training, but the fact cannot be denied that a military pilot is trained to be prepared for risks, whereas a civil pilot should be trained to avoid them.

My bureau was progressing slowly but surely. It did not make a lot of money: I had not expected it to. But I had built up an index system that was daily proving its worth. As specialists of all types were on my registers, I was able, in addition to my normal commercial business, to give a great deal of help to ex-Service pilots and men who were searching for jobs. Knowing how little the Services were then doing to place these men in civil employment, I always had a soft spot for them. When I heard later that the Air Ministry was considering the formation of a special department to assist officers retiring from the R.A.F. to find civil employment I tried to interest them in my work and suggested they might care to employ my services. Sir Sefton Brancker advised me to make an appointment with the head of the Air Ministry's education department, who was then handling this subject. The interview I got proved useless, and it was obvious there would be no chance of co-operation.

But other people were becoming interested in my bureau. Mr. R.M. Balston, a founder member of the Royal Aeronautical Society, and Mr. F.R. Nutting offered to turn my concern into a private company. Mr. Balston, who knew Sir Sefton personally, thought it might be possible to obtain his co-operation, and, after we had verbally agreed on the terms of a contract between us, he had an interview with the same head of the education department who had turned me down. At first the interview appeared to be successful, and it was understood there would be co-operation with "Merriam's Aviation Bureau". But, until that interview, it had been agreed that I should hold the controlling rights. After the interview my prospective partners were unwilling to concede this – I can only guess why. As I, after all, had done all the spade work, I could not accept my loss of control, and so the plan fell through.

Finding it increasingly difficult to keep pace with the work of my bureau in London and wanting to spend more time with my family, I moved my headquarters to Whiteley Bank on the Isle of Wight. It meant a decrease in business but afforded me a better chance of keeping my health.

I had not been long back on the Island before I stumbled on a fresh opportunity to establish a gliding school. Passing through Newport one day I noticed a placard advertising a meeting to be held in the Guildhall to consider the formation of a gliding club. The organizers were J.B. Smith of Ryde, and H.R. Coward of Carisbrooke. I was so interested that I decided to attend and take my wife. With us came Capt. F.L.M. Boothby, R.N., and together we sat at the back listening to the speakers. As usual, everyone who spoke was optimistic generally, but hesitant in making concrete suggestions. And so the proceedings dragged on in a vague atmosphere of goodwill until someone mentioned my name. Then, before we realized what we were doing, Boothby, my wife and myself were on our feet making enthusiastic speeches. When my turn came to be heard I told the meeting that my previous efforts to start gliding on the Island had failed, but that I still had my original glider – with "birds now nesting in its wings", which could easily be reconditioned and made airworthy. I added that, if there were sufficient persons interested, I would be prepared to place it at the disposal of the club. But I believe it was my wife's enthusiasm more than anything else that inspired the meeting to action. She described from her own experience the fascination and exhilaration of gliding and related how much I had learnt about it while watching the seagulls hovering and soaring in the up currents near the cliffs. She ended by saying she was certain that, once they had tasted the delights of this sport, they would never lose their enthusiasm for it.

A week later a further meeting was held at Whiteley Bank at which a firm decision was recorded to form a club. The Mayor of Newport, Mr. H.V. Horan, presided and was enrolled as our first member. Sixteen other persons were also enrolled, and I was elected captain, with Mr. J.B. Smith as hon. secretary, and Capt. Boothby as hon. treasurer. To get the club going I offered it the temporary loan of my old school premises and glider as well as free supervision of instruction.

Sir Sefton Brancker was to have come down to open our club, but had to decline at the last moment. This was the last I ever heard from him, for shortly afterwards he was killed in the airship R101. With him perished also Lord Thomson, Major Scott, and many other well-known aeronauts. The news of this disaster came as a shock to the whole nation, and those of us who knew these men personally were much affected by their loss.

Our club began to flourish, and we soon had enough members to be able to buy another glider – a Lowe-Wylde (Figure 47), known as a B.A.C. – which was delivered to us by Mr. Lowe-Wylde himself. Major C.W. Brannon, M.C., a founder member and a son of the proprietor of the County Press, did so much to publicize and thereby increase our activities that eventually we were able, with Sir Alliott Verdon-Roe's permission, to extend them to the Saunders Roe airport, Sir Alliott himself then becoming our President. Among the other eminent people whose interest we attracted were the Hon. Ernest Guinness, whose pilot, Capt. Ellison, made a number of glides with us, Capt. Balfour, M.P., and the sons of Mr. John Lord, then a director of Saunders Roe. In all at that time we trained about forty members to fly, including my daughter, Rosalind. In addition to supervising I kept our instruction up to date by frequent visits to the clubs on the mainland, and Herr. Kronfeld, whose sensational glider flights had won him fame on the Continent, was induced by the efforts of Lord Sempill to come to Dorset to demonstrate.

When I see the interest our Government now takes in gliding and think of the early struggles we went through to get recognition, I sometimes wonder if it will always be so. Will the pioneers always have to struggle on doing the spade work, mastering seemingly insurmountable difficulties and often spending far more than they can afford?

Wishing to extend my bureau activities and realizing that Southampton was destined to become a premier flying base, I moved there with my bureau in 1932. So as further to extend its activities I formed the bureau into a company and began to concentrate more on the industrial side. I also became the sole British agent for two well-known makes of American light planes under hire purchase agreements. Shortly before the last war I was taking part in negotiations for the establishment of a light plane factory near Eastleigh airport in conjunction with several Southampton business men, who included Commander Bird, R.N., of Vickers, a director of Cunliffe Owen's and others. Not wishing to become too rusty, now I was taking on this new business, I arranged with Mr. W.L. Gordon, manager of the Hampshire Light Plane Club, for a refresher course in modern methods. My instructor was K.C. Winton, a very experienced ex-R.A.F. pilot, and, after two or three flights on a Gipsy Moth, I was flying solo again and amazed to discover how quickly my old touch had come back. While there I was more than pleased to meet Bill Dunning, the Club's chief engineer, and to find that he used to help the Roe brothers with their machines in Manchester in 1910.

With the gathering of the war clouds in the late summer of 1938 I offered myself for service on the Reserve. In the meantime, while I was waiting for a reply and the nation began at last to prepare for the conflict, my bureau register proved most useful in supplying badly needed aeronautical engineers to the Fleet Air Arm at Southampton and Lee-on-Solent. When the war came I was invited, through the good offices of Rear-Admiral Bell Davies, V.C., to join the Fleet Air Arm in an advisory capacity with the rank of Lieutenant Commander. Accepting this offer with alacrity, I closed down my business, leaving my wife to clear up the details while I plunged wholeheartedly into the Second World War.

Chapter 21

Back in Navy Blue

The Germans began to take up gliding not many years after the First World War. They pursued and expanded its development with such determination and rapidity that all those who saw in gliding not merely a sport, but also a valuable preparatory training for pilots of powered aircraft began to suspect their motives. By 1936 it was obvious to all thinking persons in the world of aviation and to some outside it that the real reason for an activity so greatly encouraged and helped by the Nazis must be its value for war purposes. I myself, as I have related earlier, had consistently and strongly advocated the encouragement of glider flying in Britain so that we, too, could build up a large reserve of men who would need the minimum amount of training to prepare them for duty as military pilots.

During all those years leading up to Munich it seemed that, whichever Party was in power, H.M.'s Government was determined, like the three monkeys in the fable, to "see no evil, hear no evil and speak no evil". Germany's example and the warnings of our own men appeared to pass unheeded, and even Munich, when it came, did not seem to awaken our authorities to the full seriousness of our position. When I took up my duties at Lee-on-Solent under Admiral Bell Davies I was amazed to find how unprepared we really were. But, while it appalled me, it also spurred me on. My task there was to sort out applicants for the Fleet Air Arm according to their capacity for its various duties, and I was happy in the realization that at fifty-nine I was still young enough to enjoy doing such an important job of work. It was one I knew from A to Z, for, since 1926,

111

the business of my bureau had largely consisted of advice to youngsters on the branch of aviation for which they were best fitted, and I had evolved a system of tests that were almost uncanny in their accuracy. Never before had I worked so hard on the ground. The enthusiasm of the young volunteers of 1939 was itself an inspiration to work. If only our Governments had been moved by the same enthusiasm in the years before the war, how different our position would have been.

Before I had been at duty a month I was struck by the haphazard and rather academic method of selection employed by the Fleet Air Arm and the waste of human material it entailed. It seemed to me that all we did was to see that the candidate was physically fit, ask him a number of questions, accept a given standard of education or the results of written or oral tests, and then pass him for aircrew duties. This method lacked the indispensable practical element, and, as a result, many would-be pilots and airmen were being grounded after fairly extensive periods of training because they were found deficient in that vital thing – air sense. My tests at the bureau had been mainly practical. They incorporated many of the tests subsequently employed by American selection boards and, indeed, by our own psychiatrists; but there was an essential difference. In training over a thousand pupils to fly under conditions which would have made the present-day instructor's hair stand on end I had come to know the type of pupil who would be likely to succeed and the one who would probably kill himself through slowness of reaction or over-confidence. I could spot, too, the one who would be slow to learn, but who would probably make the best pilot in the long run.

It may well be asked how it was that I thought I could pit my opinion against the accumulated skill of the Service selection boards. In my business I had to know; mistakes meant loss of business and of reputation. That was one reason. Another was that I had a great sympathy for those many applicants who could not pass certain of the tests and yet who were, I recognized, suitable for training nevertheless. After all, if I had been put through a medical board and selection board in 1911 I should never have been allowed to fly, and yet I started to fly at thirty-one with partially defective vision and literally fought my way against medical opinion to the front rank of peace- and war-time instructors. When all the factors that go to make or mar a pilot are closely examined it will be discovered that by far the most important one is the man's determination to fly. If a man has that determination – that longing to be in the air – then, I say, he can overcome many things that might otherwise disqualify him.

When I thought the time was ripe I submitted to the Admiralty a plan whereby I should categorize applicants after applying my own tests, even to the extent of advising on their suitability for training as fighter, bomber or other type pilots. I had tried these tests in conjunction with Mr. J.E. Doran Webb of the Wiltshire Flying Club and several others. All of them told me that the pupils I had recommended gave hardly any trouble to teach. I now demonstrated them before Admiral Bell Davies, Surgeon Captain E. Shaw, Commander K. Smith and other officers, all of whom were most enthusiastic. I also explained to them that the introduction of my methods would, I felt sure, much reduce the number of hours spent in flying training.

The question of the best method of selecting pilots was to prove a battle throughout my war service. My ideas were always received, duly noted and then on one pretext or another, quietly filed away. The Service preferred, it seemed, to rely on "experts", who in turn relied on accumulated statistics, but those who really understand statistics know how dangerous they can be. According to statistics we should never have won the war, but we did.

My ground job, it seemed, was likely to prove at times almost as exciting as my previous war service had been. Though I was fortunate not to be at home when my garage and car were destroyed by a bomb that just missed my house, I was on the air station at Lee-on-Solent shortly after the fall of France when we were first bombed. Hearing the planes approaching before the sirens sounded, I gave the warning to the M.O.s and their staff who were in the building. We all rushed for the shelters and reached them only just in time. The first bomb set the sick bay and the M.O.'s car ablaze, and soon the hangars and machines around us were burning fiercely. Even in the air raid shelter the heat was like a furnace. The most exasperating thing about this raid was to see how weak our defences were against the enemy's relentless attack. The gunners did their best, but they were no match for the Germans. What would I not have given for even an old Nieuport Scout with a machine gun firing through its propeller. Say what you like about anti-aircraft guns, the best way to deal with bombers is by attack from the air. Any bomber pilot will tell you which he fears most. As a result of this disastrous raid, in which many were killed and wounded and much damage done to the station, we were supplied with a flight of aircraft for defensive purposes. One of the pilots of this Flight was that same Esmonde who was later awarded a posthumous V.C. for his heroic attack on the "Prinz Eugen" when she escaped through the Straits of Dover. Another staff pilot at Lee-on-Solent was Lieutenant, now Sir, Ralph Richardson, R.N.V.R. With him were two of my 1915 pupils, Lieut. Stevens and Lieut. Commander C. Haliphide, the latter being one of the survivors from the aircraft carrier "Courageous".

One of the terms of my engagement with the Fleet Air Arm was that I should stay at Lee-on-Solent for the duration of the war, and I was therefore somewhat surprised when I was asked to take over selection board duty at H.M.S. "Royal Arthur", a training establishment at Skegness. As I had packed up my house at Southampton and moved my family to Lee, I was not at all keen to move, but, in view of the importance of the work, I did not demur. Sorting out the hundreds of applicants for ground and air trades at Skegness, I was, if possible, busier than ever before. It was while here that I had the honour of being introduced as "one of the pioneers of the air" to the Duchess of Kent.

As the tempo of training increased I was moved again, this time to H.M.S. "Duke" at Malvern. Here I served under Capt. Spencer-Cooper, R.N., and soon came in close contact with Service psychologists. Whatever may be thought about psychologists generally, and admitting that they have done and are doing useful work for the Services, in my opinion their value to the Services is apt to be vastly over-rated. If one took the official view one would imagine that, without them, it was well-nigh impossible to select suitable candidates; whereas most of us in the Service know that the best judges of a man's ability are those who have been through the mill themselves and who know from their own experience what type of man is wanted for what type of job. Men whom I interviewed complained to me of the methods being employed by the psychologists, particularly the paper tests; and when some were turned down I was at a loss to understand why. I even took the trouble to make a special visit to one of the most prominent London psychologists to find out the why and wherefore of their methods. While there, I asked him to test my methods, and, after over an hour's close examination, he confessed that, not only were my methods thorough and exhaustive, but that he could learn a few things from me. This was certainly flattering and gave me just the encouragement I needed to continue my fight. I would not have minded so much if the psychologists had had some knowledge of the trades for which the men were volunteering, but they had not, of course. Some of the men they turned down even came with references from civilian firms which certified their ability at the bench.

What with the commotion I was making about these selection boards and my frequent letters to the Admiralty, I was not surprised one morning when I received a signal giving me three days' notice to proceed to an appointment in Jamaica. As the terms of my engagement precluded overseas service, I could afford to disregard this notice, and, as an indication of how far away some people would like to see me, it made me smile. But Fate was on the side of Authority. In the middle of this controversy I met with an accident which sent me off to hospital. While on duty one night I stumbled into a form in a darkened gangway and fell so heavily that I was unable to get up for a few minutes and found that I had severely injured my shin. When receiving treatment in hospital it was decided that I must also have a general overhaul. As a result of this I was told to go before a medical board, and not long after I was boarded I received a notice from the Admiralty regretting I was unfit for further service.

In my deep disappointment at this decision I found some consolation in the great concern and sympathy of my colleagues at H.M.S. "Duke". I particularly appreciated a letter from the padre, in which he wrote: "We all lament your departure. Of course, the whole thing is a tragedy. You endeared yourself to everybody here who is worthwhile, and it is so splendid to hear the chiefs and petty officers asking all about you and where you have gone and what you will do."

And so, deprived of any further chance of service, I finally left the Fleet Air Arm and put away the blue uniform I had worn through so many strenuous years in both wars. Sick at heart, I went home to try to bring to life again the business I had closed down three-and-a-half years before.

Chapter 22

Past, Present and Future

It is indeed a pleasant sensation when scanning the breakfast newspaper to read of the achievements of some great man and to be able to say to yourself or to your family "I remember him when he was a youth learning to fly. He was one of my pupils." Now that I am mainly an onlooker, when this happens, as it so often does, I look back on my life and think how very worthwhile it all seems to have been. With each name I can usually connect some very human incident. It is well that we should remember that those even in the highest places are only human, and that beneath the urbane exterior of success there often lie tumultuous memories of bygone struggles and defeats. But best of all is to realize that you, too, are remembered by those former colleagues and pupils who have now achieved fame. This, I am glad to say, has been my happy experience, and this it is that has so helped to sweeten the dull days since my retirement.

I shall never forget the letters from Air Marshals Sir John Higgins, Sir Patrick Playfair and Sir Richard Peirse. Sir John wrote from India, where he was the R.A.F. C. in C, and Sir Patrick wrote from R.A.F. H.Q. in France inviting me to come over and "have a look". Sir Philip Joubert de la Ferte succeeded Sir John in India and was himself followed by "lucky" Peirse. All these four men, it will be remembered, were among the first of the R.F.C. pilots who flew to France at the beginning of the First World War. Air Marshals Goble, Leckie and McKean – early Chingford pupils and then employed in the Canadian training scheme – also sent me messages of goodwill. It was while directing this scheme that Sir Dalzell McKean sent a letter of reminiscence in which he said: "There was far more thrill and sheer joy in flying in those days" (meaning Chingford), "we all knew so damn little."

It was about this time that Air Marshal Sir Leslie Brown, a 1915 "Chingflier", wrote of Jack Alcock's favourite trick at Eastchurch in those days of flying till dusk and then finishing his landing run right in the doorway of the hangar so that the mechanics would not have so far to push it in. (Enough to get you "hung" these days.) Sir Leslie also reminded me of an amusing contraption built by an engineer officer called Fowler to test pilots on engine faults. He mounted a Gnome engine on a stand and so fixed it that, when a handle was turned, there was a loud clicking noise to represent the imaginary firing of the cylinders. By another ingenious arrangement one or two of the cylinders could be cut out. On this dummy pupils had to pass a test in which they had to indicate when the engine was missing and which cylinder was at fault. By this means he probably saved several accidents, for in those days, if a low powered (and most engines then were low powered) engine missed on take-off, it was touch and go with the pilot.

Not all my early pupils now dead were killed in action. Air Commodore H.C. Brackley met his death while bathing in South America, and Squadron Commander Sir James Bird was killed by his own gun while walking in his grounds at Wickham. Sir James, together with the late R.J. Mitchell, chief designer to the Supermarine Aviation Works, was closely connected with the success of the Spitfire.

Since I taught him to fly at Chingford in 1916 until he was killed ferrying a machine for Air Transport Auxiliary, Capt. H.K. Horsey of Imperial Airways had flown 1,690,000 miles without a major accident and without injury to a single passenger. Horsey's colleague, Capt. E.J. Bailey – also a pupil of mine – retired to Tasmania in 1948 after setting up a record of 15,000 hours in the air, mostly on marine aircraft. He became the first captain of the Canopus, forerunner of the famous "C" class flying-boats, and was awarded the Air Efficiency Medal. Writing to me recently, he said: "I am thinking of putting up kite balloons here to ensure that no noisy aeroplanes come flying around."

Of my 1915 pupils, probably the most brilliant was the man who later became Air Marshal Sir John Linnell. He was knighted by the King in North Africa during the last war and was the first man to be knighted by a king on the battlefield for 400 years. On his return from Africa Sir John invited me to meet him at the Air Ministry, but, when I arrived there, I was told that he had just been killed in a jeep. As I had spoken to him on the telephone only a short while before, this came as a great shock.

Sir Philip Joubert, whom I have mentioned earlier as one of my 1912 vintage pupils and a regular broadcaster during the last war, used to maintain that enemy bombers could not be identified by sound alone – or words to that effect. I was amused, for, while it might have been true of human beings – although, like many others, I thought it was not – my little dog was never wrong. Though he did not budge for British aircraft, he would whine and dive under the table long before the sirens sounded for "Jerry".

These men whom I have just mentioned and those of whom I have given some account earlier are some of the many whose names still greet me from time to time as I read my morning paper, but I now leave personalities to attempt a general review of aviation since I first took a part in it way back in 1911 and for a few words on the future.

Apart from my forty-three years' connexion with aviation, what other qualifications have I for writing about its past, present and future? First, I can claim to have taught flying to two hundred naval and military officers and civilians before the First World War – a record at that time. Secondly, I introduced methods of instruction which were eventually copied and practised by every instructor until the advent of new equipment changed their practice but not the principle behind them. Lastly, by teaching these methods to those two hundred men I trained, I feel I can justifiably claim to have laid the flying foundation of one-third of our Air Forces of today, but I must admit that I was lucky in the beginning in having the right type of men to teach, men of character and ability who could profit by my methods and pass them on to others.

In making any criticism I have one further advantage – I can't call it a qualification – in that, now my flying days are over and I am out of the "hurly-burly", with no axe to grind, with no capital to endanger, and with no powerful patron to offend, I can look back over the years and gaze at the present day with an impartial eye.

The first thing that strikes me as I review the past is that flying owes more to the moral qualities of faith, courage and hope than it does to knowledge and skill, whether human or technical. In the beginning it was these qualities far more than anything else that made flying possible. Though not in the same degree, they are still needed; and, I suggest, they will never entirely cease to be needed while flying progresses. In saying this I am not belittling the splendid work of our inventors and designers. To their brains and skill aviation owes more than it can ever repay, but if these men look into their hearts I think they will agree that what sustained them most in achieving their successes was faith, courage and hope.

This account of my working life has been chiefly a record of the sacrifices and achievements of men struggling with the unknown, and it has paid, perforce, little attention to the help given to them by machines and technical developments. In this short space I can describe only one of the many mechanical inventions and improvements that have helped to make flying what it is today. It is the Gnome engine (Figure 50). I choose this particular machine not only because of its technical merits but also because it arrived at a crucial stage in the history of aviation. Invented, I believe, by M. Seguin and produced about 1910, it was of a revolutionary design and created almost a revolution in the progress of flying. Until its advent almost every aircraft engine was a heavy, water-cooled affair of much the same type as those used in motor-cars. Whether water cooled or not, they all had a low "power-weight" ratio; in other words they were heavy for the amount of power they produced. And few of them were at all reliable. Now, at this stage in flying, weight meant everything, and we had reached a point when progress was being held up by the difficulty of finding means of increasing power without unduly adding weight or increasing unreliability. The main revolutionary element in the design of the Gnome was the fact that, whereas in the motor-car engine the cylinders are fixed and the crankshaft revolves, in the Gnome the crankshaft was fixed and the mass of the engine with the cylinders revolved around it. Arising from this cardinal principle were two important features: a smaller crankshaft and no necessity for water cooling. The cylinders were fitted with radial fins, and the engine was cooled by the mere rotation of the cylinders through the air. Together, these two features gave what everyone was looking for – a higher power-weight ratio. And the engine was, for those days, very reliable. The merits of the Gnome were rapidly appreciated, and by 1913 there were about five times as many aircraft fitted with Gnomes as those with any other type of engine. In August 1914, half the aeroplanes which flew to France with the R.F.C. were powered by these engines. Technical developments, especially in the science of metallurgy, later caused the rotary principle to be abandoned, but instructional aircraft fitted with Gnomes were doing useful work up to 1918. Aviation indeed owes an immense debt to M. Seguin.

Private enterprise gave birth to flying. Private enterprise, backed by public support, brought it through its childhood. The First World War hastened its growth to adolescence, and, with the First World War came complete Government control. Though private enterprise after the First World War once more played a considerable part in the progress of aviation, Government control had come to stay, and, with the advent of the next war, the needs of a Government representing the will of the nation again became paramount. Now, nearly nine years after the last war, when aviation has reached a robust manhood, we find that private enterprise is almost entirely dependent on Government support and is therefore to a large extent controlled by Government. For this the two wars and the continuing demands of our Fighting Services for the present "cold" war are largely responsible. Had it not been for these wars our present position might be very different, but it has not come about solely through wars and control from Whitehall. I suggest that another cause is the ever-increasing tendency to think of everything in terms of the people considered as a whole, rather than in terms of the individual men and women who go to make up that whole. In civil aviation this has produced a sort of elephantine growth of larger and faster and costlier air liners demanding ever larger and better and costlier airports, a growth to which the humble desires of the ordinary man and woman seem to be almost entirely subordinated.

Many a man who would like to experience the joys and thrills of real flying is not willing or cannot afford to indulge in the dubious pleasure of being sealed in an air-tight cabin in which he is passively hurled, at a height so great that he can distinguish little below him except the difference between land, water and cloud. It is true that we also have great liners to take us across the sea, but for the man who wants to experience the pleasures and perils of the sea or to use it for his lawful occasions we have craft of every size and kind from a two-oared rowing-boat upwards. There is no real reason why we should not have the same kind of facilities, though not quite so abundant and cheap, for the man who wants to fly for pleasure or profit. Had it not been for the wars and the spread of the disease called "nationalism", I believe we should have them now.

As things are now, the ordinary man of some substance or earning a fair income has come to regard the possibility of private flying for himself as so hopeless that he just does not bother to contemplate it. The first remedy, the one I have preached and practised so often – though mainly for another reason, is more glider and light aircraft clubs. At first they may need support from public funds. There could be few worthier and in the long run, from the national point of view, more profitable uses for them. Later, when the movement spreads, as it is bound to, and private flying becomes commonplace, subsidies will no longer be needed. For individual flying there is no need for large and costly or even small and not so costly airports. There is no need for this purpose to have expensive helicopters. If there is a demand for them, many an existing aircraft firm could turn out sturdy light aeroplanes capable of taking off from and landing in low-hedged pastures not more than 150 to 200 yards long with speeds up to 80 m.p.h. and costing under four figures. Such fields could soon be found or made near any town. And don't let us be led away by the lure of high speed. Averaging only 70 m.p.h. I could leave by air from Southampton and be in Exmouth in an hour and a half, a journey that would take three and a half by road and four by rail. In the event of trouble such aircraft could make a safe landing almost anywhere *en route.* A man who is keen will soon learn to service his own aircraft and find it no more difficult than looking after his car.

When I write about the joys and thrills of "real" flying and compare the present with the past I realize, somewhat sadly, that much has been lost. Light aeroplane enthusiasts will experience much of them; Service pilots may taste them for a few brief hours during their early training; but most of those who are handling modern machines are not enjoying all that flying has to give them. To get the most out of being in the air or on the sea you must feel yourself to be a part of that element. We cannot become birds, nor can we yet hope to experience the intense joy of those winged and feathered beings of the far distant future that Olaf Stapledon so vividly describes in his *First and Last Men*, but in an early Avro or

B.E. with their open cockpits or even in an old box-kite with no cockpit at all we were far nearer the birds and those feathered beings than a modern pilot is in a Vampire or Sabre. The glider man knows what I mean, and so does the man at the helm of a sailing dinghy or small racing yacht. We were a part of the air and subject to its whims and caprices, but we could turn and twist in our own length, land sideways, land like falling leaves, land round corners, land close to our own shed, tuck ourselves away in a small field or on a narrow beach and get away again unaided, and all the time we were flying we felt the clean air whistling past us. Modern air liners, bombers or fighters have to come to ground under outside control and with much of the care, preparation and organization that attends the docking of a "Queen Elizabeth". Dignified and responsible, but give me a sailing dinghy or a "Bluebottle" or an early Avro to handle every time.

In advocating the fostering of far more glider and light aeroplane clubs and the development of private flying I am not prompted solely by the wish that more people shall be led to enjoy a thrilling experience. As I mentioned in the course of my narrative, I had, and I still have, a more serious purpose. Every day it becomes more apparent that the chief defence of these islands must rest with the Air Arm. The Navy, sad to say, can no longer be expected to guard us alone, but let us take a lesson from the way the Navy built up her strength in the days when it was our main bulwark against attack. The chief source of our Navy's strength was, and still is, our large, skilled and hardy seafaring population. Nowadays, of course, it also draws on our large industrial reserves of skilled artisans and mechanics, but without the men of the sea and that sea sense most of us islanders inherit from the day we were born it would not be the magnificent fighting machine it is. If we are going to be great in the air, as we must be if we are to survive as a great nation, we must make our people air-minded and build up a large reserve of men with air experience. The best and cheapest way of laying the foundation of this reserve is to develop glider and light aircraft flying. The gap between the man in the street and the pilots of first-line fighting aircraft is daily becoming wider as the machines grow more complex. We must see that everything is done to narrow this gap. There should be gliding clubs on the outskirts of every town and light aeroplane clubs near every city and large borough.

Designers and constructors must also be encouraged, by subsidy if necessary, to build cheap and efficient small aeroplanes for the private flyer. The money can be found if our Government takes its courage in both hands and ceases to provide medical treatment and spectacles for every foreigner who visits our shores. If more money is needed, let us save the millions we spend on grandiose projects like "ground nuts" and the Brabazon. To my mind the Brabazon scheme is typical of that mania for size and a spurious prestige that has infected our leaders. How many clubs could have been established and equipped with their small gliders and aeroplanes with the millions we have wasted on this monster.

We are apt to look at our modern achievements and marvel at the progress that has been made, but we must be careful that in admiring what has been done we do not make the mistake of assuming that every new thing is a step forward in the right direction. Though private enterprise is still the moving factor behind our advance and might by itself be relied on to supply or anticipate our real needs, when subject to political control and the theories of ideologists who are more concerned with abstractions than realities, it is sometimes led to strive for wrong or secondary objectives. Aviation as a whole has certainly made amazing progress in the last forty-five years, and that progress has been so rapid and spectacular in certain directions that the man in the street and many who should know better have been dazzled into believing that all is well. All is not well. In the last fourteen or fifteen years aviation has advanced only on a relatively narrow front. In these years progress has been almost entirely technical, and the technicians have concentrated almost exclusively on two main objectives – speed and size. This would not be a matter for concern if other aspects of aviation were satisfactory or were not being neglected. We should be fools if we concentrated on men-of-war and transatlantic liners to the exclusion of all the other vessels and small craft that ply the seas. If it is retorted that aviation finds no demand, except for very limited and special purposes, for other types of aircraft and facilities, I would reply that in the beginning no one would have demanded boats with sails until they had seen what boats with sails could do and had been trained to use them. Perhaps the growth of flying has been unduly forced by world conditions. Be that as it may the so-called progress of modern aviation is entirely in the hands of specialists and experts who, encouraged and supported by Authority, pursue purely technical and specialized aims. It is the duty of informed writers and the Press to explain to the Public not only what is being done but also what could and should be done in the air. That duty is not being fulfilled. One day men will be projected through space from the earth to the moon. It will be sad if, when that day comes, only one man in ten thousand can fly himself through his native air from one part of the earth to another.

On this note I end my memoirs, hoping that they may have helped to fill some of the gaps in the history of aviation. This book is as much a plea for the individual as it is a record of events. It is a plea that in this age of more and more centralization we shall make certain the individual is not forgotten and that his voice shall be heard with a sympathetic ear. That, after all, is the basis of our democracy. If we lose that, then we lose all that is worthwhile. Flying was begun by individuals. We must see that it is not entirely taken from them by Governments and Corporations.

Index

Abbott, Major C.R., 78
Abbott, F.O., H.G., 28
Abdullah, 24
Accidents, 40, 49, 64, 70, 76-7, 85, 117
Aerial photography, 92
Aeroplane, The (quoted), 15, 79, 105
Aircraft Display, The "£5W", 41
Air Efficiency Medal, 117
Airship R101, 108
Airships, 42, 92-4
Alcock, Jack, 33, 55, 56, 97, 115
American Flying Corps, 49
Anderson, Lieut. E.V. (killed), 20
Anti-submarine patrols, 82, 84, 87, 92, 94
Anzani aircraft engines, 8
Ashford, Lieut. A.E.N., 94
Ashmore, Gen. R.E.B., 24, 25, 70
Atkinson, Lieut. (R.F.C.), 54
Atlantic, first crossing of, 33, 55, 87
Australia, first flight around, 74
Autogiro, 100
Avro 504 (aeroplane), 10, 11, 38, 62, 71, 82, 105, 121, 122
Aziz, 24

Babington, Col. J.T., 95
Baby Hamble Scout plane, 83, 84
Bailey, Capt. E.J., 117
Ballooning, 42
Balston, Mr. R.M., 107
Bannerman, Major Sir A., 17, 27
Barnes, 9
Barnes, D.M., 70
Barnwell, Capt. F.S., 37

Barnwell, R.H., 24, 25, 31, 37, 41
Bauman, F.-Lieut. E.B., 56
B.E.2c (plane), 68, 70
B.E.8 (plane), 55
Beadle, Mr. P.H., 99
Becke, Capt., 30
Beevor, Lieut. Frank, 37
Bendall, W., 26, 36, 43
Beta Dirigible, 41
Biggs, Mr. J.G., 5
Billing, Mrs., 16, 44-5
Billing, Pemberton, 38
Bird, Sq.-Com. Sir James, 56, 109, 117
Bird of Passage, the (plane), 10
Blackburn aeroplane, 11, 13
Blackburn, F.-Lieut. N.W.C., 71
Blackburn, W.-Com. Harold, 17, 100
Blackburn, Robert, 11, 13
Blériot, Louis, 7, 12
Blériot monoplane, 12, 40, 62
"Blimp" airships, 92-96
Blue Bird Restaurant, Brooklands, 16, 21, 44, 45, 51, 55
Blundell, Lieut. A.H., 94
Boger, Lieut. (R.F.C.), 24, 54
Boothby, Lieut. F.L.M. (R.N.), 41, 108
"Box-Kite King", the, 34
Brabazon aircraft, 123
Brabazon, Major the Hon. Claud, 23-4, 25
Brabazon, J.T.C. Moore-, 7, 9, 10, 17
Brackley, Air Commodore H.G., 74, 97, 113
Brancker, Sir W. Sefton, 37, 101, 105, 107, 108

Brannon, Major C.W., 109
Brett, R. Dallas, *History of British Avia-tion, 1908-14* (quoted), 32, 47, 53
Brewer, Griffith, 7
Bristol, 5
Bristol "Bullets", 62
  Flying school, 13, 40, 47, 51, 81
  monoplane, 20, 25, 30, 46,
  "pusher" biplanes, 14, 17, 24, 25, 32, 41
British and Colonial Aeroplane Co. (now Bristol Aeroplane Co.), 7, 32, 33, 37, 44, 51, 53
Britannia Trophy, 30
Brock, Commander (R.N.), 70
Brock tracer bullets, 70
Bromet, Air Commodore C.R., 47
Brooklands Automobile Racing Club, 20, 27, 35, 36
Brooklands Flying School, xi, 7, 10, 12, 17, 18, 22-3, 30, 31, 32, 37, 41, 44, 45, 46, 47, 51, 55, 61, 62, 71, 78, 79, 81, 96, 101
Brown, A. Roy, 73, 76, 77
Brown, Air Marshal Sir Leslie, 117
Brown, Whitten-, 97
Buckingham Palace Road, London, 6
Buckland, F.-Com., 84
Bulkeley, Lieut. H.I., 20
Burleigh, Bennett, 42
Burt, Petty-Officer (coastguard), 94
Busteed, Harry, 23
Butler, Mr., 78

Cadbury, Mr. E., 56
Callaghan & Co., London, 40
Callaway, F.-Lieut. W.B., 87
Calshot, 82, 90, 99
Campbell, Lindsay, 25
Canopus, 117
Cantacuzene, Prince, 23
Carmichael, Lieut. (R.F.C.), 24, 54
Carwardine, Dr. T., 49
"Cathedral", the (aeroplane), 12
Cattewater R.N.A.S. Station, 82-6, 87, 93
Caudron biplanes, 26, 45, 56
Central Flying School, Upavon, 39, 46, 49

Channel, first crossing of, 7
  first crossing by an Englishman, 11
Charlton, Capt. L.E.O., 37
Charteris, R.L., 17
Cheeseman, E.W., 24, 27
Chingford Aerodrome, 37, 61-67, 69, 71-3, 76-8, 80, 82, 94, 116, 117
Christie, Lieut. A., 20, 54
Churchill, Sir Winston, 59
Cierva, Juan de la, 100
Cinquevalli, Paul, 3
Cockburn, Mr. G.B., 13
Cody, Col. S. Franklin, 11-12, 42, 43
Cogan, Lieut. (R.F.C.), 54
Coleman, J.P., 56
Connah, W.M., 79
Consuta plywood, 99
Convoys, escorting, 84, 86, 87-8, 92, 93
Cooper, Capt. Spencer, 114
Cork, Mr., 46
Courtney, Capt. Frank., 100
Coward, Mr. H.R., 108
Cox, Sir Reginald, 6
Croydon, 29th Training Squadron, 51, 96
Cull, Lieut. J.T., 48
Curtiss aeroplanes, 42, 49, 64, 94

Daily Mail, 7, 22, 97, 100, 101, 106
Dallas, Major R.S., 32, 47, 53, 79-80
Darley, Lieut. C.C., 43-5
Darracq, Mr., 24
Dartmouth, 91
Davies, Rear-Admiral Bell, 110, 111, 113
Deane, Sgt. E.N., 50
De Dion cars, 4, 6
Deperdussin monoplane, 56, 69
De Havilland, Geoffrey, 10, 43, 52
De Havilland planes, 57, 78
Delacombe, Mr. H., 7
De Ville, F.-Com. E.A., 94
Ding, Mr. Rowland, 63
Don, Midshipman D.S., 51
Dowding, Capt. Hugh, 37
Driscoll, Col, 34-5
Duke, H.M.S., 114, 115
Dunne, J.W., 9
Dunning, Bill, 110

Eastleigh Airport, 109
Elder, Capt. W.L., 65, 66
Ellison, Capt., 109
England, Geoffrey, 30, 47
England, Gordon, 18, 30, 101
England, H., 40
Esmonde, Lieut., 114
Evans, Capt. L.P., 43
Ewen, Major W H., 22, 47, 100

Fairey Aviation Co., 52
Fairey C.R., 33
Farman, Aeroplane, 55-6
Farman, Henry, 10, 38
Farman, Maurice, 56, 76
Farnborough, 20, 30, 41, 42, 45, 54
Fazil, 24
Fellowes, Lieut.-Com. P.F.M., 74
Fethi, 23
Field, R.M., 56
Firle Beacon, 101
First World War, 10, 22, 26, 35, 37, 45, 47,
    52, 53, 54, 58, 79, 87, 93, 101, 111, 116,
    118, 120
Fisher, Mr. Frank, 100
Flanders, Howard, 105
Fleet Air Arm, 110, 111, 112, 114, 115
Fleming, 16
Fokker, Herr, 101
Fokker triplane, 76
Foster, Lieut. MacNeece- (R.N.), 54
Franklin, Benjamin, 11

Galpin, F.-Lieut., 76
Gamage, Mr., 4
Gardner, Charles, 106
Gaskell, Major Penn- (R.F.C.), 54, 70
Gates, F.-Lieut. R.T., 56
Gaudron A.E., 42
Gerrard, Capt. E.L., 13
Gerrard, F.-Com. T.N., 60
Gibbs, Sir Philip (quoted), 71
Gilmore, Graham, 35
Gipps, G. Lancelot, 48-9
Gipsy Moth planes, 110
Glanville, Lieut. (R.F.C.), 24, 54
Glen, J.A., 77
Gliding, *Daily Mail* Competition, 100

Gliding School, Whitely Bank, 102, 106
Gnome aircraft engines, 14, 20, 26, 27,
    48, 119-20
Goble, Air Marshal L.E., 74, 116
Gordon, Mr. Douglas, 102
Gordon, W.L., 109
Gorell, Lord, 10
Gould Brothers, of Exeter, 6
Gould, Mr., 24
Gould, Lieut. C.G.S., 25
Grace, C.S., 17
Graham, R., 56
Gravenell, Mr., 99
Gregory, Lieut. R. (R.N.), 12
Grey, C.G., 79
Grey, Spencer, 59
Griffin, Lieut., 49
Grosvenor, Lord Edward, 39-40, 44, 63
Groves, Commander R.M., 56, 58-9, 65
Guinness, Hon. Ernest, 109

Halford, F.B., 45
Haliphide, Lieut.-Com. C., 114
Hall, J.L., 27
Hamel, Gustav, 22, 28, 36
Hampshire Light Plane Club, 109
Handasyde, G. ("Handy"), 105
Handasyde, Mrs., 29
Handley-Page aircraft, 56, 61, 62, 63, 66
Hanlon, Lieut., 24
Harker, F.-Lieut. M.A., 76
Harvey, Lieut. J.D. (R.N.), 46
Hawker, Mr. Harry, 12, 28, 51, 97
Hayward, F.-Lieut. C.H., 76
Helicopters, 121
Henderson, Gen. David, 17
Henderson, Lieut.-Col. G.O.P., 98
Hendon Aerodrome, 12, 26, 40, 52, 54,
    55, 56, 58, 60, 61, 65, 66
Henson aeroplane, 7
Hewlett, F.E.T., 18
Hewlett, Mrs. Maurice, 18, 102
Higgins, Air Marshal Sir John, 21, 31, 54,
    116
Hoare, Sir Samuel, 105
Hodsoll, E.J., 56
Hodson, Mr., 101
Holt, Air Vice-Marshal F.V., 95

Hope, Dr. Allen, 49
Hope, Lieut., 24
Horace "Shorthorn" planes, 9, 33, 78
Horan, Mr. H.V., 108
Horsey, J.F., 74
Horsey, Capt. H.K., 117
Hosking, Lieut. (R.F.C.), 54
Hotchkiss, Mr. E., 19-20, 22, 23, 24, 25, 26, 47
Houston Everest Expedition, 74
Hucks, Mr. B.C., 11, 22, 43

Imperial Airways, 74, 117
Influenza epidemic (1919), 95
Issy-les-Moulineaux, 12

Jackson, F.-Lieut. G.H., 76
Jamaica, 115
Jones, Mr. Vernon, 40
Joubert de la Ferte, Air Marshal Sir P.B., ix, 23, 25, 30, 54, 116, 118
Jullerot, M., 35, 46, 47, 52

Keane, Pte. (Padstow coastguard), 94
Kehrmann, Lieut. J. Crawford, 40
Kemp, R., 17
Kerr, General Mark, 95
"Kittiwake" amphibian plane, 99
Knight, 28, 37

Lambe, Commander C.L., 65
Lane, F. Sub-Lieut. H.P.D., 87
Lavigne, F.-O. L., 80
Leckie, Air Marshal, 76, 77, 116
Ledeboer, Major J.H., 100
Lee-on-Solent, 110, 111, 114
Legion of Frontiersmen, 34
Lehmann, Capt. Talbot-, 94
Lewis, Lieut. (R.F.C.), 54, 77
Linnell, Air Marshal Sir John, 117
Lloyd, Major Lindsay, 27, 32
Longcroft, Air Vice-Marshall C.A.H., 17, 19, 30, 54
Longmore, Lieut. A.M. (R.N.), 12
Loop the loop, first man to, 35
first Englishman to, 11
first passenger to, 40
Lord, Mr. John, 109

Loultchiff, Lieut., 24
Lowe-Wylde glider, 109
Lowther, Major the Hon. C.W., 33
Lucas, J.B., 49

McClean, Mr. F., 12
alights on the Thames, 13
MacDonald, L.F., 40
MacIntyre, 74
McKean, Air Marshal, 116
MacLean, Lieut. A.C.H., 13, 42
Maitland, 42
Malvern, 114
Mander, Mr. Lionel H., 100
Maneyrol, M., 101
Manning, W.O., 18
Manston R.F.C. Station, 82
Manton, Marcus, 56, 90
Mapping, 92
Marconi Wireless Station, Poldhu, 5
Marsh, Lockwood, 10
Martinsyde aeroplane, 29
May, Mr. Fred, 100
"Mayfly" (airship), 9
Medina River, 98, 99, 105
Mehned, Ali, 24
Mellor, G.M., 95
Merriam, Mr. Olin Lane, 3, 4, 94
Olin (Jun.), 104
Rosalind, 109
Warren, 1, 4, 15, 19, 24, 47, 72, 73-4, 83, 88-9
Merriam-Newman gliders, 102
Merriam's Aviation Bureau, 107
Merrick, Major J.C., 39
Michelin tyres, 4
Miles, F.G., 105
Mills, Lieut. (R.F.C.), 54, 76
Mitchell, F.-Lieut. J.C., 76
Mitchell, R.J., 117
Mitchell, Lieut. W.G., 37
Montrose, Scotland, 30
Moore, Sq.-Leader York-, 93
More, Major Gilbert (U.S.N.), 96
Morgan, F.-Lieut. L., 76, 77, 80
Morgan, Lieut. T.W. Mulchay, 43, 54
Morrison, Sub.-Lieut. J.S., 69
Mullion R.N.A.S. Station, 92, 93

Murray, Cecil, 41, 55, 64, 72, 75, 76

Newman, Mr. G., 100
Nieuport Scout (plane), 113
    sea-plane, 82
Noel, M. Louis, 40
Nutting, Mr. F.R., 107

Ogilvie, 7
Ogilvie-Wright glider, 52
Orton, Major R.E., 94, 96
Osbourne, Brig.-Gen. H.P. Smyth, 95
Ossulston, F.-Lieut. Lord, 82

Padstow Flying Station, 94, 95
Page, Mr. Handley, 38
Paine, Capt. G. (R.N.), 46, 80
Paine, Mr. Scott, 100
Parfitt, 55
Parker, J. Lankester, 37
"Parsival" airship, German, 41
Pashley Bros., 28, 40
Patterson, Mr. Compton, 100
Payze, Capt. A., 24
Pégoud, M., 35
Peirse, Sir Richard E., 116
Pendlebury, W.M.F., 35, 49
Percival, N.S., 18, 26
Perrin, Commander H.E., 10
Perry, Lieut. Copland, 55
Petre, H.A., 18
Pickles, Sidney, 31
Pierson, R.K., 37
Piffard, Harold, 9, 42
Pigott, Sub-Lieut. J.R.W. Smyth-, 48, 49
Pixton, Mr. Howard, 17, 63
Pizey, Mr. Collyns, 14, 15-16, 17, 19, 95
Playfair, Sir P.H.L., 24, 25, 54, 116
Poldhu, Marconi Wireless Station, 5
Popham, Major R. Brooke-, 17
Porte, Sq.-Com., 55
Powell, Capt. D.W., 31-2
Powell, Richard, 44-5
Preston, Col. R.L., 105
Prestwick Airport, 76
Pretyman, Lt.-Col., 24, 54, 96, 100
Price, Capt. C.L., 24, 27
Psychologists, 37

Pulford, Air Commodore C.W.H., 62, 90

R101 (airship), 108
Rabagliati, Lieut. C.E.G., 52, 54
Radley, James, 41
Rae, F. Sub-Lieut., 74
Raleigh, Major G.H., 17, 54
Rawlinson, A., 17
Raynham, F.P., 18, 28, 97, 101
Read, Lieut., 31
Redpath, R.F., 77
Reid, F. Sub-Lieut. H.V., 77
Renault aeroplane, 29
Reveria, H.M. Aircraft carrier, 91
Reynolds, Lieut. F.H., 95
Richard, Lieut. L.F., 51
Richardson, Sir Ralph, 114
Richthofen, Baron M. von, 76
Robertson, Lt.-Col., 76
Robertson, Lieut. E.D. Maxwell, 47
Robertson, Major F.A. de V., 79
Robinson, Capt. Leefe, 70
Robinson, Lieut., 45
Roche, Lieut. (R.F.C.), 54
Rodwell, Capt. M. (R.F.C.), xi, 54
Roe, Sir A.V., 7, 9, 10, 18, 109, 110
    triplane, 17,
Roe, E.V., 98, 110
Rolandi, Lieut. V.A.F., 94
Rolls, Hon. C.S., 9, 17
Royal Aero Club, 7, 10, 17, 48, 50, 54, 97,
    105
    Accidents Committee, 49
Royal Aircraft Factory, 42, 45
Royal Air Force formed, 94
Royal Arthur, H.M.S., 114
Royal Flying Corps, 11, 40, 71
Royal Naval Air Service formed, 12

Sahni, 24
St. Nicholas' Home for Crippled
    Children, Byfleet, 35
Salaries, instructors', 22
Salmond, Capt. W.G.H., 37
Sampson, Lieut. C.R. (R.N.), 12
Sandown, I. of Wight, 98, 105
Santa Claus, the first Flying, 32
Saunders, Sub-Lieut. F.G., 48

Saunders, Capt. K.F., 77, 102
Saunders, Mr. S.E., 99, 105
Saunders-Roe Airport, 109
Schaak, Herr, 41
Schneider (Sopwith) Scout planes, 84
Scott, Lieut., 94
Scott, Major, 108
Scriven, F. Sub-Lieut. V.R., 87
S.E.5 (plane), 76, 79
Sea-plane joy flights, 97-103
Sea-plane School, Cowes, 105
Seaview, 105
Second World War, 42, 57, 92, 110
Seed, F.-O. Randolph, 77
Seguin, M., 119, 120
Sempill, Lord, 109
Shaw, Surgeon Capt. E., 113
Shekleton, Lieut. (R.F.C.), 54
Shephard, Lieut. (R.F.C.), 54
Short balloon, 41
    biplane, 10, 39
Short, Horace E. 33, 78
Short, Oswald, 10, 33, 42
Short sea-planes, 84, 87, 89
Shott, Lieut. H.H., 25, 54
"Silver Streak" (aeroplane), 10
Sippe, 28
Sitwell, Sq.-Com., 58, 59
Skegness, 114
Skene, R.R., 40, 43, 44, 45, 54
Smith, Henry White-, 38
Smith, J.B., 108
Smith, Commander K., 113
Smith, S.E., 17
Smythies, Lt. B.E., 51
"Sociable" Dual-Control plane, 48
Sopwith Camel (plane), 76
    1½ -Strutter (plane), 92
    Schneider Scouts, 84
    Tabloid (plane, 51
    tractor biplanes, 20
Sopwith, Sir. T.O.M., 12
Spence, Capt. (R.F.C.), 54
Spencer, 28, 59, 114
Sprigg, Mr. Stanhope, 106
Stapledon, Olaf, 121
Stelling, Major, 41
Stevens, Lieut. (R.N.), 114

Strain, L.H., 43
Stringfellow, John, 7
Stutt, 52
Styles, Capt., 24
Sueter, Capt. Sir F. Murray, 41, 55, 63, 64,
    75, 103, 104
Suffragettes, 41,
Summerfield, S., 24, 27
Supermarine Aviation Works, 117
Sykes, Lt.-Col. Frederick, 17, 33

Taube aeroplane, German, 61
Thomas, Mr. (of Sandown), 98
Thomas, Mr. Holt, 52
Thompson, Lieut. (R.F.C.), 54
Thomson, Lord, 108
Tiger Moth training plane, 57, 77
Todd, Lieut. (R.F.C.), 54
Torquay, 91
Training, results of insufficient, 34, 75
Travers, F.-Lieut. Ben, 57, 70, 76
Treeby, Lieut, 29
Treloar, Mr. Harold, 52
Trenchard, Lord, 12, 46, 54, 102
Trevelyan, G.W., 52
Triumph motor-cycle, 4
Turner, Major C.C., 33, 41, 42, 100
Turner, Lewis, 63

U-Boats, 84-5, 87, 88, 89, 93
Upavon, Central Flying School at, 39,
    46, 49
Usborne, Lieut.-Com., 42

Valentine, Jimmy, 54
Vaughan, Capt. C., 78, 105, 106
Vickers Flying School, 37, 38, 40, 47, 53,
    97
Vickers monoplane, 41
Vickers tractor plane, 40
Voigt, Herr Willy, 46

Wadham, Capt., 95
Walcott, Capt. H.E., 47
Waldron, Lieut., 54
Wallace, "Tubby", 73
Walley, Mr. Sam, 4
Wanklyn, Lieut. F.A., 24, 25

Warlow, Capt. W. Picton-, 43
Warneford, Sub-Lieut., shoots down
   Zeppelin, 56, 58-9, 63, 64
Waterlow, Lieut. (R.N.), 41
Waterlow, Major, 42
Watkins, F.-Lieut. A.B., 82
Watkins, Lieut. H.E.M. (R.N.R.), 48
Weaver, Mr., 101
Webb, J.E. Doran, 113
Wertheim, Princess Lowenstein, 63
West, Capt., 82-3
Wheeler, Midshipman N.F., 27
White, Sir George, 53
White, Mr. (of Bristol Aircraft Co.), 51-2
White, Mr. Claude Grahame-, 54, 56, 73,
   80, 97
White, Samuel, 90
Whitely Bank, 107
   Gliding Club, 108
   Gliding School, 102
Wickham, Mr. R., 100, 117

Wightman, C.M., 79
Willis, Mr., 46
"Willows" R.N. airships, 42
Wilson, Lieut. C.W., 20, 52
Wilson, S. Corbett-, 42
Wiltshire Flying Club, 113
Windsor, Duke of, 51
Winton, K.C., 110
Wood, Capt. T.H.F., 17, 40
Wright, Frank, 28
Wright, Howard, T., 9,
   "box-kite" plane, 12, 42
Wright, Maurice E.A., 52
Wright, Orville, 6, 7
Wylde, Mr. Lowe-, 109
   glider, 109

York, Duke of, 96, 100

Zeppelin raids, 45, 58, 62, 63, 68-74, 76